POLICY AND PRACTICE IN EDUCATION
NUMBER TWENTY-ONE

PROFESSIONAL SCHOOL LEADERSHIP,
DEALING WITH DILEMMAS

POLICY AND PRACTICE IN EDUCATION

POLICY AND PRACTICE IN EDUCATION

SERIES EDITORS

JIM O'BRIEN and CHRISTINE FORDE

PROFESSIONAL SCHOOL LEADERSHIP, DEALING WITH DILEMMAS

Daniel Murphy

Headteacher, Lornshill Academy, Alloa
formerly Director of the
Centre for Educational Leadership,
University of Edinburgh

DUNEDIN ACADEMIC PRESS
EDINBURGH

Published by
Dunedin Academic Press Ltd
Hudson House
8 Albany Street
Edinburgh EH1 3QB
Scotland

ISBN 978-1-903765-75-3
ISSN 1479-6910

British Library Cataloguing in Publication data
A catalogue record for this book is available from the British Library

Typeset by Makar Publishing Production
Printed in Great Britain by Cromwell Press

CONTENTS

SERIES EDITORS' INTRODUCTION

Policymakers determined to put the case for a particular initiative often seem to overlook the real challenges they present to the practitioners charged with implementing these policies in school. Often the successful implementation of particular policies rests on the ability of school leaders to balance competing needs and demands as they introduce the new initiatives into school. In this book the experience of a professional school leader provides insights into the very real dilemmas faced by school leaders charged with putting policies into practice and suggests sound ways of dealing with these.

Daniel Murphy draws widely from sources in philosophy and psychology as well as in education and management to explore the experiences of school leaders in dealing with dilemmas for which there is no simple solution. In this book he builds up different levels of understanding of what dilemmas are: from an exploration of the emotions that surround dilemmas, to an examination of the micro-politics of a school which can influence decisions to, finally, a more considered approach based on an understanding of dilemmas within an ethical model. With this ethical framework, Daniel Murphy creates a very practical tool for school leaders. He draws widely from his considerable experience as a school leader to provide several illustrative vignettes which illuminate the nature of dilemmas whilst suggesting ways of using the ethical framework to resolve these. Ultimately, as the author clearly demonstrates in his discussion, dealing with dilemmas cannot and should not be avoided in schools. As part of the educational process we, as educators, should seek open and ethically sound ways of discussion to help resolve the dilemmas that arise inevitably within an increasingly diverse society.

Dr Jim O'Brien
Vice Dean and Director,
Centre for Educational Leadership,
Moray House School of Education,
The University of Edinburgh

Dr Christine Forde
Senior Lecturer in Educational Studies
The University of Glasgow

ACKNOWLEDGEMENTS

The project which resulted in this book began when, as a practising head-teacher, I struggled to articulate what seemed the biggest challenges of the job. There are many people who have taught me by their example, by their courage, by their integrity and humour, by their insights: too many to mention them all individually. Prominent in any list would be the parents, pupils and staff of the very different schools in which I have been privileged to work as headteacher: Crieff High School, McLaren High School and Lornshill Academy. I have learned a great deal from many headteacher colleagues, including those who shared time and insight to support my research. It was inspiring to work alongside some first class university colleagues during my time at the Centre for Educational Leadership, in particular Jim O'Brien, Janet Draper, Linda Croxford, Lindsay Paterson, Jennifer Kerr and Jim Fleming (the latter two having read and offered typically insightful and rich comment on various drafts of sections in the book). Pamela Munn and David Carr also offered helpful suggestions and support on the project at an earlier stage. Students on various programmes were an unfailing source of inspiration: the teacher always learns more from the students than the other way round. I also felt warmly supported by the wider academic community, whose insights and understandings underpin anything worthwhile contained in this slim volume. Particular thanks are due to Jackie Dunlop whose comments were very helpful, while Christine Forde is an unfailingly supportive and understanding editor. At home, my wife Joan and my family have tolerated excessive intrusions into family life over the past year, as I tried to write around a busy work and domestic schedule. While this work depended on all the above, to all of whom I am extremely grateful, mistakes and errors are entirely my own.

For the family, friends, colleagues and students,
whose insight, care and support have meant so much to me.

Chapter 1

DILEMMAS, DILEMMAS ... AND THEN SOME MORE DILEMMAS ...

This introductory chapter explains why I wrote this book, and why I believe it makes a worthwhile contribution to our understanding of the role of the headteacher[1] in the contemporary school and, more widely, to our policies and practices in school-based education. It also outlines briefly the structure and rationale of the book that follows.

Why this book?

I took up my first post as a headteacher in 1992 in a state secondary school which served a rural community in Central Scotland, following a successful early career as a teacher and local authority adviser. In 1996 I moved to become headteacher of a larger secondary school with a wider and more comprehensive catchment. Although judged by Inspectors to show 'very good leadership' in both schools, and although there were many achievements to be pleased with as I worked hard with the school communities involved, my experience of school leadership (i.e. what if *felt* like to be a headteacher) was not at all straightforward. Indeed, there were many tensions and emotional pressures for which I had had little preparation so that I often felt highly challenged by areas where it seemed there could *never* be success. I experienced, for example, a constant tension between what was expected of me by employers and what seemed possible or even desirable in the schools in which I served. The new managerialism of the age had led to a growing sequence of requirements on the 'what' and the 'how' of school practice. Heightened public expectations of the educational systems expressed itself in a series of bold and ambitious aims for comprehensive schools in Scotland, typical school aims stating that the school would 'respond to every child's needs and ensure that every child reached his or her potential'. Meanwhile the complexities and challenges of young people growing up in a more individualistic and plural society constantly bulged out of the neatly ordered boxes into which national guidance, or a school's limited curriculum, declared that they should fit – and it seemed that many expected me, as headteacher, to *make* them fit into these boxes.

Although these were the experiences of a Scottish school headteacher, they were echoed in the experience of many others, in other places.[2] These tensions could also be found in other school sectors. As a secondary school headteacher (in Scotland most secondary schools are comprehensive schools for children aged 11–18), I was often envious of the greater degree of cultural and social homogeneity of the primary, special or nursery school. There, a continuing ethic of placing the 'child at the centre' together with a less complex bureaucratic structure, seemed to create the conditions for a stronger agreement across the school community about key values and priorities. However, there were tensions in the other sectors too. Many primary headteachers found the framework of the Scottish '5–14' curriculum (SEED, 2000b), with its prescriptive attainment targets and sequential programmes of study, restricted their ability to respond as they wanted to what they saw as the needs of their pupils. Although team relationships in the Scottish primary schools I knew were generally very good, if they did fall apart then the fallout could be much more intense. In one example of a rural primary school with only one class of pupils, the teaching headteacher had 'fallen out' with a parent who supplied half the school roll (a large family!). In a small rural community where both lived, this created enormous personal and professional tensions for the headteacher. Although much of the international research quoted in this book, and much of my experience, refers to the secondary sector, I therefore believe many of the issues and points made have a relevance to many in other school settings.

Preparation for the role of headteacher in the Scottish system when I was first a headteacher in the early 1990s was both limited and poorly conceptualised. As a group, practising Scottish headteachers got on with the job, as best they could, though they had not been introduced to the concepts, the analyses, the professional understandings which would allow them to understand and respond to these tensions. As a practising headteacher seeking the space to talk about and understand the job through wider reading, it was therefore a liberating experience to come across the voice of Gerald Grace (1995). Looking principally at the impact of government reforms in England, and linking into broader debates about government and public service, he contrasted the oversimplistic educational prescriptions of 'managerialism' with the wider set of understandings about school leadership present within the international professional community of educators. A key point was that headteachers needed access to a range of conceptual resources which would help them to understand and interpret the complexity of what happened in their own school, where they had to act.[3] In my experience the urgent complexity of daily life in a school community had seldom represented itself in the generalisations of university-based research, focused towards analysis and description rather than advice on how to act. Nor did the interest-based negotiations of national policy committees, with their carefully worded compromises, help guide action. The model projected in official Scottish policy documentation (HMI, 1988, 1989, 1996) was of the headteacher as 'efficient manager', working to a predictable pre-ordained script which would automatically lead to success. If you followed the formula, everything would be fine. However, I seldom met a headteacher who felt that this was the case. The experience of headship was of a discontinuity between the generalised advice of official policy and the urgent often reactive character of life in a school community. There, complexity replaced simplicity; difficult conflicts of interest replaced clear rational decision-making. In this indeterminate environment, headteachers were often expected to mediate and make decisions – and, working without the intellectual resources Grace argued for, found it difficult (O'Brien *et al.*, 2003).

I found myself in a position of growing conflict with my bosses in the local authority in which I worked (they did not appear to share my view of the indeterminacy of much school life, tending towards a formal managerialist view) and hemmed in by the restrictions of national curriculum guidance (which limited teachers' abilities to respond to children's needs). I was also frustrated by my inability as a headteacher to share my professional concerns with the civic community which I served. Most Scottish headteachers working within local authorities are governed by strict rules on what they can say and to whom. All concerns over the impact of poor policy making have to be fed through the line manager, usually in Scotland a local authority director. Often the differing bureaucratic and political priorities of the post prevent the director, who has a duty to defend the local authority in any public forum, from fairly representing the impact of policy on the delivery of the service. I believed that the public, in particular parents with children at school, needed to know about some of the policy problems which prevented teachers in their schools from doing their best for their children. My tentative sallies in that direction (Murphy, 1999) had met with restrictive cautions from my employer, who did not welcome public discussion of this kind. I, on the other hand, was anxious to contribute both to the civic debate which I believed was needed and to the intellectual development of the profession. I was therefore pleased in the year 2000 to take up a post at the Moray House School of Education in the University of Edinburgh, to deliver the Scottish Qualification for Headship or SQH (see Reeves *et al.*, 2002) for a fuller analysis of SQH), the newly instituted training framework for aspirant Scottish headteachers. SQH offered access to international best practice models, encouraged school leaders to think professionally about their role and not to view themselves as 'branch managers' and, above all, it provided a wider set of concepts and criteria to help understand and interpret the tasks than the overly simplistic statements of some official policy.

My role within the university expanded to that of Director of the Centre for Educational Leadership, a Centre whose ambitions were to expand understanding of the role of school leaders through research, conferences and publication. In this role, I expanded my own research activities and through my teaching and training sought to explore the less determinate and more complex world of the *experience* of school leadership, an experience that often seemed at odds with the 'theory'. This book is the outcome of some of that research and teaching experience, seeking to summarise and explain some of the messier bits of school leadership and to provide a map, and some signposts, of the territory through the concept of dilemmas.

The concept of 'dilemma'

The concept of 'dilemma'[4] does a good job in encapsulating many of the difficult and messy experiential aspects of school leadership. These are situations where a choice has to be made but where, no matter what you chose to do, you appear to go against a key value or leave one of the people or groups involved in the situation aggrieved and unhappy.

In a small-scale research project I conducted to open up to view these aspects of the work of the school leader (Murphy, 2002), a set of dilemma vignettes (similar to those below) acted as a stimulus to semi-structured interview and focus group discussion. Experienced headteachers who took part showed a strong degree of association with these examples which 'encouraged empathy', and had been 'typical', part of the 'day to day' of school life, 'close to my experience', 'particularly appropriate to my experience'. 'I empathised with them all.' Headteachers involved in this study went on, unprompted, to identify a wide range of other dilemmas they had experienced, beyond those outlined in the vignettes. This Scottish experience was not untypical. Important studies of the experience of headship conducted in several school systems in the late 1990s (Day *et al.*, 2000; MacBeath, 1998) independently identified dilemmas as one of the key experiential features of headship. According to Day's research team, 'together the constructs of 'tensions' and 'dilemmas' capture the immediacy of the continuing conflicts faced by many heads in the study' (p. 134).

Cuban (1992) identified dilemmas as a defining characteristic of the role in his wide experience and research in the USA.[5] He pointed out that 'we seldom examine these below-the-surface conflicts even though we cope with them continually in our work. We call them pesky problems or brush them aside as peripheral to our core business of getting the job done' (p. 6). Yet, he argued, they are far from peripheral. They are part of the 'genetic code' of the job (Cuban, 1996).

Other studies across a wide range of educational systems quoted below have framed their research using the concept of 'dilemmas' to capture an important part of the experience of headship. In an example of recent research in the area, Ehrich *et al.* (2006) reinforced the perspective that such dilemmas are at the heart of the school leaders' professional experience, one of their respondents memorably stating that ethical dilemmas were 'really the bread and butter of what school leaders do'(p. 111). This study framed dilemmas as being essentially ethical in character.

Duignan and Collins (2001) use both an ethical and a political frame in reporting. Their extensive study was carried out across four professional groups in Australia (the Service Organisation Leadership Research Project). Since more than 1,000 were surveyed and over 100 interviewed, while more than 500 took part in website debate, the volume and quality of data generated by the study is exceptional. The investigators discovered a range of tensions at the heart of leadership practice – tensions which were categorised as in Table 1.1 below. In looking for explanations for these tensions, Duignan paints a picture of turbulence in the Australian context, quoting a survey by Little (1997) in which top leaders complained that 'desperational change', driven by global and technological forces, was squeezing 'aspirational change' out of the picture.

Table 1.1 Tensions of contemporary leadership
(after Duignan and Collins, 2001)

1	good of the community	vs	rights of the individual
2	loyalty	vs	honesty
3	service	vs	economic rationalism
4	status quo	vs	development
5	long term	vs	short term
6	care (individual)	vs	rules (consistency)
7	values (articulated)	vs	practice (what is done)

Moller (1996), in a study of the work experiences of school superintendents and principals in Norway, found that those she studied were strongly oriented towards action rather than reflection, often prioritising their time towards situations of conflict where their actions and decisions could resolve the situation. However, given space and a structure within which to reflect, something they did not readily do in the busy work environment, they often 'described their actions in everyday practice as a choice between different sets of dilemmas. The dilemma was a concept that captured the contradictory orientations they experienced where there were no right answers. Each course of action carried its cost and benefit' (p. 212).

This book contains a number of real life examples from Scottish schools of these commonplace complex conflicts which caused great anxiety to the headteachers involved, presented here as anonymised vignettes. The first two follow here. In each case, it seems to the headteacher that she or he is trapped between two or more equally unpalatable course of action: a classic dilemma. Such dilemmas are not unique to school headteachers. Many of the issues of emotional and ethical challenge involved in experientially based accounts of headship practice can be found across the teaching profession, and other caring professions, and also in many accounts of management practice in private as well as public sector organisations. However, there are specific situational issues to explore in the headteacher role.

Vignette 1

A school, following national advice, is implementing a healthy eating policy, including a ban on fizzy drinks and certain types of sweets in school and significant changes to school menus. Every day, four vans, selling chips, burgers, ice cream, fizzy drinks and sweets park outside school at lunchtime and are doing an increasing trade. The vans do not just pose a threat to healthy eating, as there are road safety risks as well as worries about other anti-social activities in the crowded pavement area beside them, with unemployed local youths mixing in among school pupils, bringing drink and possibly drugs. Because it is a public pavement, the headteacher has no authority there and has received no proactive police support, as they only react to incidents. The headteacher tries to 'ban the vans' but gets no support, either from the local authority which has issued trading licences to the vans, or from parents, more than half of whom, despite clear warnings about their children's safety, sign letters stating that they would like their children to visit the vans at lunch-time. Ignoring their presence is not an option, as the headteacher believes that they present a very bad image of the school, while she also believes there to be a risk of a serious incident (personal safety or road safety) if things carry on unaltered.

Different politicians, locally and nationally, are responsible for different aspects of this situation – healthy eating and trading standards. Parental priorities (access to choice at lunchtime) are different to those of national government (healthy eating). Many pupils in the school prefer fatty, heavily salted foods. The headteacher is left with the messy consequences of the partial responsibilities of other decision makers and feels responsible as well as accountable for these, even though she would never have created this situation herself, given the opportunity and responsibility to develop a coherent policy that worked for the school. Although the main problems may be seen as political (conflicting policy priorities and different sources of political power – democratic power and consumer power), the varied perceptions and values of the individuals who share responsibility for this situation clearly play a role in creating the headteacher's dilemma. Should the headteacher accept any responsibility for the situation?

Vignette 2

A local authority has established a special support service for children whose first language is not English. This service provides advice and support to schools, teachers, families and children. In the middle of the summer term, one of the advisory teachers left the service and has not been replaced. Children in a particular school who received regular support from the service no longer do. The headteacher discovers after summer that a new teacher has been recruited but is being used in a high profile reception centre to support asylum seekers. She argues with her director that she needs to have the service restored, as pupils in her school are suffering. However, she is told very clearly that the other service is a very high political priority and that the resource must go there. She is not aware of a great deal of public debate on this issue and believes that the wider civic community should have the chance to discuss the decisions made and their consequences. Some of her pupils are being disadvantaged and only she is really aware of what an impact that is having on them. She wants to contact the local press to inform them, and through them the public, but knows that this will break standing instructions which do not permit her to discuss any aspects of local authority policy with the media.

In terms of her own values and what she believes to be in the interests of her pupils, the headteacher feels she should be 'whistleblower', but also acknowledges that she has no right to speak directly to the public and her conscience will not let her do this through covert means. She is frustrated that in a matter of such civic importance as education, the voice of the headteacher is muted. She feels that the minority ethnic community children who are no longer getting support have been an easy target for 'cuts' because they have no political voice. She becomes very personally wound up about this tension to the extent that it colours her experience of work. She considers resigning. Once again, there are several challenging factors involved here – emotional, political, ethical.

Even experienced headteachers may find these kinds of conflicts difficult. For trainee headteachers, this is almost always the case. In the Scottish Qualification for Headship programme, for example, trainee headteachers analyse and reflect on 'critical incidents' in their developing practice (Tripp, 1993). Often these incidents could be described as classic 'dilemmas'. However, in my experience the characteristically reactive reflections of the trainees on these critical incidents, although valuable, frequently lacked a theoretical base and located the source of the dilemma in the people involved, or in a personal failure of management skill, without linking the individual experience within a broader framework of understanding or analysis. How the dilemma is framed is a central feature of its potential resolution.

Key themes

Despite the very wide range of international studies using the concept of dilemmas, there is no clear and universally adopted analytical categorisation. There are, however, some strong common themes, themes which resonate with my own reflective experience of headship and which provide the content of the next three chapters:

- Dilemmas are interpreted conceptually and experienced emotionally (Chapter 2).

- Dilemmas often arise in a school environment which is socially and politically complex (Chapter 3).

- Dilemmas involve values, so ethical frames of reference are required to understand them (Chapter 4).

Creative and imaginative insights into dilemmas is the stuff of drama and tragedy, but aesthetics has been sacrificed in this book to the demands of a study framed in the academic tradition (see Walker and Shakotko, 1999; Best, 1999;McFall, 1998).

Chapter 5 has a practical focus. It builds on the understanding developed through the three analytical perspectives of the earlier chapters. Advice is offered on how the headteacher can over time reduce the incidence or intensity of at least some of the dilemma situations. It also models a 'toolkit' for responding to dilemmas. This toolkit explores the 'best possible' (or sometimes the 'least unacceptable') solutions. Chapter 6 goes on to examine the wider implications of the insights gained for our understanding of schools, school leadership and, more generally, public service in our complex society. Although the book is written to be read from start to finish, sequentially, each chapter is designed to have a value even if read independently of the others. Academic referencing conventions have been followed where appropriate, but this is the book of a practitioner, keenly involved in the midst of professional practice, and that grounded perspective informs the text. This is not just about analysing and describing the difficulties of practice, but one which engages with the excitement and creativity of looking for solutions.

Since embarking on the book, I have returned to the messy world of school leadership as headteacher of Lornshill Academy, a busy comprehensive school in Central Scotland, encouraged by changing national policy trends in Scotland, trends which have reflected a growing appreciation of the complexity of public service and the need for local decision making. There were several significant arguments between teachers / headteachers and the political and administrative authorities who ran the Scottish school system in the 1980s and 1990s – arguments which often resulted from a lack of trust on the part of those who had to implement the changes (teachers and headteachers) of the motives of those demanding change. These arguments suffered from being interpreted as being essentially political (who has the power?) rather than administrative (can we agree what the system can reasonably achieve, given current capacity?). The Scottish examination results fiasco of August 2000, as a result of which many students received wrong results, displayed clearly the disastrous consequences of a policy community not listening well enough to those on the ground doing the job (Paterson, 2000). Subsequent developments under successive Education

Ministers have freed up local decision making, recognising the need to rebalance the relationship between national level direction and local expertise. These national policy developments made it possible for me to imagine that a school where I was headteacher could have a better stab at trying to realise those ambitious aims which it set for itself, to 'meet the needs of every child'. I would have to say that despite the changing policy context, and my enhanced awareness of the issues, the challenges and dilemmas seem as difficult and challenging as ever! The conceptual map provided here is not simple. Exploring dilemmas takes us into the complex heart of contemporary schooling. However, I hope you will find some of the resources to 'understand and interpret' for which Gerald Grace has argued, and that you enjoy reading and using the ideas in the book as I have enjoyed writing and researching it.

Notes

1 Throughout the book, the term 'headteacher' will be used as a generic term in relation to the leadership and management of schools of different sizes and types and will therefore cover 'school principal', 'school leader', 'school director'. The term also covers all those in school leadership teams who share in the responsibilities and dilemmas described, for example vice principals and depute headteachers. 'Principal' is used where this is the term used in research quoted or cited.

2 This book, and the international comparisons used, is largely based on experience and studies in the developed English-speaking countries of the world, with some reference to Northern European studies. Although the evidence base is therefore culturally restricted, the analysis has a more general application.

3 Grace makes this point with special reference to the Heads of Catholic schools and their spiritual and educational inheritance, but it has a more general application.

4 Dilemma: '(a) a situation involving choice between two equally unsatisfactory alternatives; (b) a problem seemingly incapable of a satisfactory solution' (*New Penguin English Dictionary*, 2000).

5 Cuban's research and experience also lead him to see 'dilemmas' as an important characteristic of the work of superintendents (local directors of education), as do Grogan and Smith (1999) and Moller (1996). Athough in this study, dilemmas will be considered largely in the context of the school, the generalisability of the concept and its application to wider areas of professional practice is a theme of Chapter 6.

Chapter 2

PERCEPTION, COGNITION AND EMOTION: THE EXPERIENCE OF DILEMMA

Dilemmas are tense and difficult situations because of how they are experienced by the individuals concerned. There are variations in how a headteacher and others involved might interpret a dilemma conceptually, what he or she sees as the headteacher's role in it, and different emotional reactions to the situation. These can affect both the situation and the potential options for resolution. This chapter explores these variations in the following sections:

- Headteachers prefer action to reflection.
- Those involved may frame dilemma situations differently.
- Perception and learning both have emotional and cognitive components.
- Some dilemmas can cause intense emotions.

Action focused

The literature does not portray headteachers as a professional group who are overly introspective, giving themselves a hard time about decisions they get wrong. Even in the difficult and complex dilemma situations, they want to 'get on and sort it'. For example, the studies conducted by Day *et al.* (2000) in England and Moller (1996) in Norway both portray school principals as people who prefer 'action' situations where their choices made a differ-ence. Moller comments that although those involved in her study took time to reflect, this was on the whole a new experience for them, one which in some cases was associated with feelings of guilt at not being available to members of the school community because of time spent in reflection. In my research with Scottish headteachers (Murphy, 2002), they were much more anxious to get on and discuss their preferred solution than to reflect on the character of the dilemma. This has also been my experience in the training situation. A workshop I have run in several programmes involved presenting dilemma vignettes (similar to those in this book), and inviting participants to discuss in groups (a) what they thought was at stake and (b) what their preferred solution would be. Almost invariably, there would be at best only limited discussion of what was at stake (or no discussion at all) and groups would move quickly into discussing the best solutions. This action focus has been seen as a characteristic of many in managerial positions, such as those Mintzberg famously described (Mintzberg, 1975), who seemed to prefer an identity in which they are too busy doing the job to stop and reflect. Gronn (2003) describes school leadership as participating in a 'new work order', characterised by work intensification, constant and inevitable overloading and short lead and response times. My 2003 survey of headteachers in Scotland (Murphy, 2003) reinforced the findings from similar surveys in New Zealand (Billot, 2003) and Australia (Cranston *et al.*, 2003) that despite high levels of job satisfaction, headteachers reported themselves as heavily overloaded. Used to continual workplace stimuli, an overload of executive and bureaucratic tasks and gaining immediate satisfaction from interpersonal relationships, headteachers seem never to have or to make enough time to stop and reflect.

Varied perceptions

In defining situations individuals vary. Greenfield (2004) states, for example:

> Despite the helpful studies to date, there remains a tremendous gap in the school leadership and organisation knowledge base – how is it that people come to understand one another and get anything worthwhile done? The field still knows relatively little about how administrators, teachers, or students actually make sense of their worlds. And surely their understanding of their worlds, the sense they make of their experience, is a critical guide to how they respond to the events and circumstances in which they find themselves.

Cuban (1996) distinguishes dilemmas from problems conceptually – problems can be solved, dilemmas cannot. My research study of headteachers' dilemmas (Murphy, 2002) suggested they can also be distinguished experientially: one person's *dilemma* was another's *problem* and was *not even* a problem for a third. One headteacher, for example, had never experienced tensions in the relationship she had with her local education authority, whereas for some of the others who had experienced dilemmas arising from such tension it was a dominating experience of their headship. Before reading on, read Vignette 3 on the next page. Should the headteacher accept any responsibility in this situation? The incident caused the headteacher who actually experienced it several sleepless nights. However, another headteacher in my research study lost not a moment over it. He had drawn very clear lines around what he was responsible for and what he was not responsible for. The original incident was outside school therefore it was 'nothing to do with him'. These different reactions suggest very different ways of looking at the same event. Rossmore (1989) argues that in thinking about a problem, it is possible to 'dilemmacise' too quickly. The first step in any situation which looks like becoming a dilemma, is to ask if the distance between the horns can be reduced.

Vignette 3

A father and mother call in to school unannounced to explain their daughter's absence. They report to the headteacher that she has been bullied and harassed sexually outside school by another student and that she refuses to come to school so long as he is there, since she may meet him in class or in the corridor at any time. Although nothing has happened in school, the emotional turmoil and personal pressure she has experienced is such that she cannot bear to see him. How could she possibly sit in class with someone who did this to her and study Maths? A complaint has been made to the police in connection with the alleged sexual offence which is now under police investigation. The parents, in tears, demand that the boy should be kept out of school, as their daughter is being punished twice, once by being assaulted then by being denied her education. The headteacher knows the pupils involved and believes that what the parents have said is probably true, but has to explain that nothing has been proved against the boy, who is also entitled to education and to the presumption of innocence. The parents become very angry. The school, they say, is failing in its duty of care to their daughter, so they will now prepare a statement for the local press explaining that the school is doing nothing to protect their daughter who is undergoing the most horrific ordeal.

In this example, the headteacher finds himself trapped between his emotional sympathy for the girl and the fact that the boy is 'innocent till proven guilty'. The intensity of his feeling is increased because the parents are holding him individually accountable for the problem. In wider society, when an accused is released on bail, or, pending trial, denies guilt, the victim and alleged perpetrator can often avoid each other through conscious decisions about movement and activities. In school, this is not possible, as both must share the same space, and there is no recognition of this problem in any policy. Both young people involved have rights and interests, but they are seen to clash.

Clearly, the individuals involved have quite different views of what is going on. To understand and respond to what is happening here, we need to explain why individuals frame events differently. The following general account of cognitive framing is based on Chambers (2003), Levinson (2003), Reyna (2002), Savile-Troike (2003) and Aitchison (2002) as useful introductory summaries of the state of current knowledge and debate in their respective fields, as well as the work of Donaldson building on Piaget and Vygotsky

(Donaldson, 1992) and the broad sweep summary of Pinker (1998). After this short summary there is a more extensive discussion of how these insights relate to the perception of dilemmas:

- In order to work effectively in the world, human beings have evolved a complex range of sophisticated ways of processing information such that the most important information draws itself to our attention urgently; often these are routinised, largely unconscious ways of processing information and judging which lead to patterns of expectation.

- The physical and social world in which we now operate is vastly more complex than the African savannah in which the physical aspects of these systems evolved; current social plurality and cultural complexity require different kinds of interpretative skill and understanding if the links between emotion, language, culture and cognition are not to be misread.

- Human beings have the potential, through complex and sophisticated neural networks, to develop complex and successful interpretative systems and to communicate these with each other through language.

- These interpretative systems or schema (unconscious and conscious, articulated in language or unarticulated but understood) provide a network of flexible and responsive ways of deciding the significance of events in the world around us.[1]

- Particularly important in linking emotion and perception is our understanding of the *intentions* of others, developed from our earliest interactions, and of the impact of their intentions and other external events on our own intentions.[2]

- We learn the schema which we use in interpreting and acting in the world in part through innate predispositions which are part of our genetic inheritance, but these are not all 'hardwired' behavioural mandates, but are often and most powerfully softwired potentiality, developed into actual skill and knowledge through experimentation and testing, both environmental and social, as we grow.

- In part, we construct our schema through linking intention and language in our infant and childhood stages. In part we develop our schema by experiments through which we are constantly testing how accurate our schema are – trying out through expressive language and through our own attempts at agency whether the way we represent the social and physical world 'fits' with the way it is.

- The social aspects of human life are related in complex ways to our communication strategies, which involve both language and non-verbal communication about culture and relationships, as well as specific bits of communication for functional and instrumental purposes.

- Reliable patterns of behaviour, predicted by learned schema, characterise much of our interaction with the natural world; as adults we encounter more dissonance in the human world when individuals have not behaved the way in which we anticipated.[3]

- As we adopt and use schema which become routinised as more or less successful ways of interfacing with the world, we develop resistance to change; our schema become bound up with our notion of our own identity – who we think we are.

- Emotions play a role in short-circuiting complex decision making processes by drawing urgent attention to events and intentions that are highly significant.

- Emotions guide our behaviour but can also be managed and manipulated.

This general account of how human beings interpret the world has obvious relevance to the 'framing' of dilemmas. Stimuli and new pieces of information are interrogated by schema to see where they fit and gaps are filled in accordance with schema-constructed expectations. A good example quoted by Donaldson (1992, pp. 91–2) is the language experiment of Bransford and McCarrell (1974) in which they confused participants with sentences such as: 'The haystack was important because the cloth ripped.' Once they subjects were told the sentence was about a parachute jump, they could locate the sentence within a sequence of events that made sense. That missing phrase provides a context for the sentence, a context of which adults in our society have some knowledge which then wraps round the sentence and provides it with an overall meaning which it otherwise lacks. Those who are experts in particular areas often have highly sophisticated flexible schema which can approach new problems with a range of conceptual tools with which to 'make sense'. Often the schema give us 'fuzzy categories' (Donaldson, 1992) which overlap and allow for a helpful flexibility in how we understand what is going on – we only seek the level of precision required for our particular purpose. We pay particular attention to those stimuli which make a difference in terms of current activity or are unusual or have implications for our agency and actions. Professional experts do not always do this in a conscious sequential way, but use tacit knowledge to fill in gaps (Sternberg and Horvath, 1999). From a different academic sphere, Schon (1987) refers to this as 'knowledge-in-action'. Headteachers and other skilled professionals may be able neither to explain to others nor to themselves how they know or understand in a certain way

(Keil and Wilson, 1999). Many schema they use have become automatised. Argyris (1990) talks of a 'ladder of inference' by which we use unarticulated assumptions to select the information from which we draw conclusions. Frequency of use in our adult lives, or learned routines from early in our developmental phase in childhood, mean that the operation of such schema is often below consciousness, not accompanied by any sense of volition and using few memory resources (Uleman and Bargh, 1989), a hypothesis given additional credibility by the difference in observed brain activity between learned and routinised mental processes and those which are part of a conscious new process (see for example Aitchison, 2002, pp. 58–60 on brain activity and language use).

However, the physical connections between schema, neural networks and the operation of parts of the brain, although an area for current neurological investigations using new techniques which suggest some very interesting possibilities, are not at all clear. Neither have psychological investigations provided a tidy map of schema in operation in their own theoretical terms. Derry (1996) suggests a hierarchy, from memory objects to cognitive fields (an activated set of memory objects) to mental models (larger strategic organising schema which attempt to make sense and interpret the bits of information). These overlap and integrate in complex ways. Much education and training is intended to influence the sophistication and the quality of the schema which we use. An unusual but interesting example is the training of naval officers to act better in crisis situations. Mental and physical routines are challenged and developed through training so that relevant information is processed correctly even in situations of great stress. In the TADMUS (tactical decision making under stress) programme of the US Navy, introduced to reduce the incidence of poor decision making in combat situations (Cannon-Bowers and Salas, 2000), trainee officers are put into pressure situations: your ship is being attacked by an Exocet missile, there is fire in the front engine room, four planes are flying towards you but you cannot establish if they are friendly or hostile. Practice in such stressful simulations helps improve processing so that the right split second judgement can be made.

Although most of us use similar highly sophisticated routines to deal with the range of complex physical and social stimuli we face, albeit in less extreme situations, we often end up with quite different accounts of the events – we pick out different features as significant. In Vignette 3, competing accounts of the events are offered. The same events are rewritten in different ways. In one (the girl's parents), an innocent girl is being twice punished, once by her assailant and a second time by the school; in the second (the boy's parents), a false accusation has been made and the boy must be presumed innocent till proven guilty; in the third, the headteacher involved wants to take responsibility and to the intervene; in the fourth, the second headteacher denies this responsibility. Only the third of these inter-pretations involves an experience of dilemma. The dissonant perceptions of the key players makes the dilemma. Resolving the dilemma must involve individuals moving from 'accommodation' to 'adaptation'. The schema with which they interpret the world must be improved. This should be home ter-ritory for headteachers. Resolving the dilemma may require those involved to see the events involved in new ways. It may require them to 'learn'. Nielsen (1996) provides an extended account based on the work of Argyris of the different types of learning which could result.

Emotion and cognition

Cognitive psychology generally has focused on how we understand and interpret what is going on around us. Yet the emotional aspects of cognition seem to provide as clear a link to behaviour. Emotions involve feelings about things that we value, and have both a physical (heart rate, sweat, blood pressure . . .) and interpretative (focusing attention, eliminating other interfering information) character. Donaldson (1992) argues that the broad interpretative schema about human behaviour typically used by educated individuals in Western cultures are unbalanced in favour of rational thinking. Too much attention has gone into our rational / intellectual development – those powerful concepts by which we seek to interpret the world as it objectively is – without giving equal attention to the modes of the mind which are concerned with locating our place in that world. We have, in this view, used our language and interpretative symbol systems to accumulate increasingly complex and technologically successful views of how the world operates, while neglecting to build our understanding of what it means to us – its links with our own agency, both in general terms (as human beings) and individual terms (in our own contexts). As soon as we move beyond looking at how we understand the world to looking at how and why we act in it, cognitive science has to be supplemented by other types of psychological understanding. Fields such as motivation move psychology into a new gear since the conscious interpretations of the individual are only one of the factors which motivate action.

Emotions are powerful, sometimes overpowering feelings that drive us on, that push us to act, that challenge or protect our understandings of our own identity. Recent psychological research shows that they are engaged in two-way processing across all parts of the brain —from motor response, to sophisticated symbolic processing – not just, as some earlier cruder versions had it, in our 'basic responses'. So what, if they are not simple primitive hangovers, are they doing there? Evolutionary psychology (this account is based on Pinker, 1998) suggests that the emotions act as powerful short-circuit messengers, prioritising for us the kinds of activities which would have an evolutionary advantage, or inclining us away from those activities which would confer no advantage. Likely stories have been offered by various biologists and evolutionary psychologists about the adaptive advantages of emotional prompts to certain kinds of behaviour. In particular the emotions – which are harder to fake than what we say – and our reading of other's emotions, help us to establish what we are really thinking or value in a situation, both for ourselves and for others. They play a role in detecting 'cheats', those who take advantage of the collaborative nature of the species by 'faking' their real intention. Emotion, cognition and valuation are, in other words, closely linked factors in our social being. In the exchanges around dilemmas, all three are likely to be found.

The 'emotional aspect' of school leadership has perhaps been under-explored and is worth further discussion here. Frequently management has been portrayed as excluding emotion ('the science of management', 'management by objectives' and so on). However, descriptions of headship practice and recent investigations into the character of successful management and leadership suggest that good leadership involves both knowledge and understanding of what emotion does and the ability to display emotional wisdom in relationships ('emotional intelligence').

A self-aware understanding of the role of feeling in balancing the impersonal rationalities of scientific management emerges from the work of Beatty (e.g. Beatty, 2000a). The difficult challenges of headship are bound to involve emotions and if badly handled, pressure and costs for the individual may impact on self-esteem, coping capacity and degree of engagement. Moreover it is the character of schools as organisations based on relationships to demand emotional engagement, not detachment. The day-to-day experience of schools and schooling involves many human interactions. Thus, those accepting leadership positions are required to undertake 'emotional labour' which can be very demanding. In the emotional intelligence research of Goleman and others (Goleman *et al.*, 2002), a high premium is placed on transferring emotionally smart leadership into a better bottom line in the company accounts. But knowing and understanding more about your emotions is not just something school leaders should do because it allows them to lead the school towards external goals. Knowing and understanding more about emotions is an intrinsic and essential part of the educational work of the school.

Headteachers in the various research studies on dilemmas generally recognise the dilemma situations as important from the emotional point of view. The issues at stake often mean a great deal to the people involved, who have invested a great deal in 'their particular view' of the events or incidents. Each one may expect sympathy and support from the head – may indeed see such emotional support as a precondition for their willingness to be involved in a resolution of the problem; they may see the headteacher's response as indicative of his or her true 'intention'.

The interplay between the perception an individual has of the situation and their position in the relative power relationships in the school community is also a factor. Feelings of powerlessness can cause strong emotion. Beatty ties her own study specifically into the frames of reference developed by Blase and Anderson (1995) to analyse power relationships in schools. Her work showed teachers' interactions with the school principal had a strong emotional character, in particular interactions concerning career. In situations where there were strong emotions at work, but these had not been surfaced and acknowledged, long-term damage could be caused:

> Teachers . . . reported that they were often misunderstood and little appreciated by their leaders, and frequently felt unknown . . . stories of harsh, public, unfair, or unwarranted criticism . . . had caused pain that was seemingly still fresh . . . When they had been humiliated by public criticism, the emotional toll had gone on for years. Some continued to suffer and to shape their professional behaviour based on wounds that would not heal . . . (Beatty, 2000b)

School leaders therefore need not only to understand but to be sensitive to the emotional impact which their power can have on others. She concluded from her research that the principal could 'have a powerful, direct and indirect influence on the growth and development of each teacher' (Beatty, 2000a): 'People will forget what you say. They will forget what you do. But they will never forget how you made them feel.'

In developing school leadership practice, headteachers are called to an understanding that leadership is not just hierarchical but relational, that isolation and suppression of emotion can be damaging, that guilt and grief can accompany situations which were badly handled and that poor relationships between teachers and school leaders can add significantly to the burdens borne by each.

A model of education which seeks student involvement, and the lifelong learning of the teacher, cannot rely on bureaucratically imposed external motivations, but must engage the internal motivation of those involved. This requires relationships of trust and respect (Beatty and Brew 2004). If key leaders within the organisation, such as school headteachers, lack the insight and skills to develop an emotionally healthy climate, then the whole organisation can suffer (Goleman *et al.*, 2002, p. 174). Goleman's work highlights how workplace relationships affect our emotional well-being and overall mood and how mood affects perception. 'Cognition only' accounts of our work experience, which give pride of place to our conceptual understanding without attention to human relationships, are insufficient. Goleman and his colleagues argue for the kind of leadership which reduces tension and stress and increases harmony and 'good feeling', a role they describe as the 'primary role' of the leader: working to produce a 'reservoir of positivity that frees the best in people. At its root the primal job in leadership is emotional' (p. ix). How much does all this add to the difficulty of the dilemma! The powerful emotions generated might destroy the trust which the headteacher is trying to build. What is at stake in the dilemma may have a very long term impact well beyond the immediate situation. The misinterpretation of the motives and intentions of the school headteacher as he or she responds to a difficult situation can aggravate and intensify the dilemma. This may not just affect the children or parents or staff involved. It can happen that the headteacher becomes intensely caught up in the emotions of the situation.

Intensity of response

A theme of personal stress, and consequent disillusionment with the job of the school principal in particular, has been widely reported in a number of studies (see for example, in addition to others quoted in this chapter, Chaplain, 2001;Evans, 2001; Mercer, 1996; Vann, (1999). In the discussion so far, the emotional labour of the headteachers has been largely seen as directed at others. Yet headteachers may be intensely personally affected by emotion in a dilemma situation. The argument above suggests that to cope with the emotional forces around dilemmas, headteachers need emotional wisdom. However, there are situations where the use of 'emotional wisdom' might not be easy, situations where headteachers are players in the game. In the vignettes given as examples here and in the research literature, the headteachers often perceive themselves to be 'in' the dilemma, not just 'managing the situation'.

First person accounts of headship (e. g. Ribbins and Marland, 1994; Mackenzie, 1995; Loader, 1997; Tomlinson *et al.*, 1999; McNulty, 2005) can be valuable in giving insight into the experience and are often emotionally charged. Those published are, however, almost always those who have 'succeeded' and may thus be untypical, although worthy, models. Aspiring and serving headteachers of less note may compare themselves unfavourably with the image of successful heads who appear to exude certainty and good judgement. These 'superheads' are popular with the media. If the successful head, an aspirant or novice might ask, is so self-assured, why do I feel pressure instead of certainty? Why do I feel I made the wrong decision, or could have handled that difficult situation better?

Bernard Barker, one of the leading English comprehensive school heads of his generation reveals this very well in his confessional account of his experiences of headship, 'Double Vision: 40 Years On' (Barker, 1999). In 1986, Barker had written an inspirational and upbeat account of what comprehensive education could and should do. By the mid 1990s, he was saying:

I was part of the problem . . . no longer part of the solution. Like so many teachers, I felt oppressed by the constant questioning of my faith. As a head, I had become an accomplice in the humiliation of teachers . . . My vision had become an ideological shell, invaded and colonised by aliens . . . a few months later they let me go. Traumatised by my 17 year Odyssey, I wondered what to do with the rest of my life. (1999, p. 82)

This is not the language of a detached management, or an intellectual spectator interpreting events from the outside, but the language of someone whose heart and soul are in the job and its mission. This is a job of feeling as well as intellect. It seems indeed that the very extent of his enthusiasm at a time of hope set up the possibility of despair as he felt trapped by the demands of the marketising reforms of national government.[4] Peer meetings in which I have taken part as headteacher often begin with what is called in Scotland 'a greeting meeting' – this is the Scots use of the word 'greeting' to mean 'crying' or 'moaning'. Only once this was out of the way could we move on to business. There was a great therapeutic value for headteachers in unburdening feelings of frustration with the tensions or problems of the job, feelings which could be expressed in the supportive atmosphere of the peer group.

Research studies show that some dilemma-type situations become so intense for some headteachers that they have the potential to damage their professional self-confidence. Whatever course of action you take as a head, you may be left with regret, or guilt, or an uncomfortable feeling that something has been lost because of your decision. Cuban (1992) reports that for those with a 'can do' mentality the messy bits left over can cause guilt, a feeling that they should be able to 'solve the problem' and a growing frustration, possibly even morale-sapping cynicism, may follow. He quotes Simon (1957, pp. 204–5) to argue that we need to be satisfied 'with what we can do', and not broken 'by what we cannot'.

In my research study, one respondent memorably stated that as a head you can be 'left with a mark because of what you have done'. Another stressed the importance of self-belief, but felt that each incident 'takes its toll'. The emotional tension of a 'public undoable job' was said by one to mean that that no headteacher could do the job successfully over a long period of time. Another talked of the physical impact if a particular problem got into your mind (lack of sleep, worry . . .). Even after the decision is made, it could 'echo' back into your emotional life. If you lost confidence in your own ability to make a decision this could get worse. In more than one case, the emotions associated with a tense dilemma of the past echoed back into the discussion itself, talking about the dilemma bringing its associated tensions back up to the surface. This vulnerability of the headteacher was commented on by several of those interviewed. Although it was not a comfortable aspect of the role, it was also seen as 'part of the territory'. One went further: 'If you are dealing with people who are hurt you have to suffer yourself.' This respondent had rejected a mentor headteacher's advice to 'grow a second skin'. Ehrich *et al.* (2006) had similar responses in their study: 'Can I sleep at night with this decision? Do I feel good in myself? It's deeply personal. I have difficulty making an unethical decision and living with it.'

Duignan (2001) uses the concept of 'The managed heart' (taken from the study by Hochschild (1983) into how feelings are commercialised), to clarify some of the emotional aspects of service in ways which provide a wider focus within which to understand the feelings of frustration of Bernard Barker and the many other school leaders who are confronted by these emotional pressures:

> Leaders . . . are expected to invest more than their knowledge and skills to effectively discharge their responsibilities in contemporary organisations. Emotional involvement and a deep commitment to their relationships, their organisation, and their work is essential if they are to be regarded as credible. (p. 35)

The ability to engage in 'emotional labour' of this kind cannot be taken for granted. All teachers in schools need the contextual and self-knowledge involved, but Duignan argues that this is a particular requirement of those who take leadership roles. He calls for 'leaders to acknowledge their own and other's feelings, emotions and passions' (p. 38).

Also recorded in the research studies are feelings of isolation. For example, Moos and Dempster (1998) found that 'internal and external priorities compete for leaders' resolution' and that 'leaders are often faced with contradiction': 'Living with contradiction so that professional integrity and self-worth are maintained is a prominent feature of contemporary leadership' (pp. 108–9). Their research suggested that 'heads are increasingly meeting these types of situations and are often left alone to manage as best they can'.

Gronn's context-setting study of educational leadership (Gronn, 2003) has provided a comprehensive structure (what he calls the architecture and ecology of leadership) within which to locate these emotional aspects of the experience. He uses quotation to define this location: 'James and Vince (2001, p. 307) describe the void between standards and practice as the "space occupied by the emotional dimension of leadership"' (p. 129). Emotional work is involved in any situation where we ensure that feelings are expressed through emotions in the normatively prescribed ways – that inappropriate expression of emotion is reduced or does not happen at all. 'Emotional labour' is the role-related commodification of feeling in the interests of job performance. It quite specifically relates to the demands of the job.

Like Duignan, Gronn argues that the requirements of New Public Management (particularly the personal identification of the success or failure of the school with the person of its head) have created heavy emotional labour demands. Gronn quotes studies of stress in headship by Carr (1994) and Cooper and Kelly (1993) to establish the high personal costs of these pressures. Feelings to which school leaders may be particularly vulnerable include feelings of failure, and the associated loss of personal identity, since so much of that identity is bound up with the work role. However, on a positive note, he also draws attention to the understudied but very important issue of humour and play in the emotions. Humour can release stress and establish connections, but can also have a negative side. It can be used to establish boundaries between 'in' and 'out' groups or, if misjudged, can expose insensitivity or a lack of sympathy. Indeed the very involvement of humour in work strategies, in 'emotional labour', could be seen as one further piece of evidence that the work intensification of recent years has become altogether too 'greedy'. Gronn uses this concept of 'greedy work' to highlight the all embracing character of educational leadership as an occupation, demanding more and more of the leader. He argues that

> the logic and ethos of work in the service sectors of increasingly service-based and knowledge-based economies, in particular the leadership of schools, represents a new form of servility . . . new forms of exploitation and serfdom which I term greedy work practices . . . Greedy work is such that it demands that one be . . . always attentive, alert, absorbed in and utterly committed to the particular task as a totally functioning, fully available, non-stop cognitive and emotional presence in the workplace . . . (pp. 147, 149)

Gronn sees this as a response to the competing and irreconcilable demands of work intensification. The demands made on the headteacher's life can only be accommodated through abandoning other aspects of life:

> Workaholicism is fast becoming the grammar or culturally accepted norm of the new work order. According to this norm, work has become an end in itself, rather than a means to an end . . . because it becomes one's life, greedy work consumes one's life, so that work becomes the measure of what one is and not just what one does . . . (p. 153)

Greedy work is a powerful concept – a workplace with a constant hunger for the worker to do more, to give more. However the headteacher reacts in a dilemma he or she may lose: intentions may be mistrusted; personal pressure may intensify.

Conclusion

This chapter has looked at dilemmas through the experiences of the headteacher. How he or she understands the situation is vital. A strong commitment to action may mean that heads do not often articulate fully their understanding of the situation. Indeed, so deeply layered may their understanding be that it may be difficult to articulate all that is involved. Hidden assumptions, poor understanding of what is at stake or of the different perceptions of the other individuals involved may reduce the options available. It is essential to bring such matters to the surface to understand the stance of the different individuals involved. In framing the dilemma it is also important to be aware of the emotional climate. The emotions of those involved colour the situation and close off or open up possible responses. The headteacher's own emotions are an important part of this. In the most challenging dilemmas, headteachers can experience intense emotional responses. While this may be a key learning point for some, studies in a number of countries tell the story of headteachers for whom an intense dilemma has been a damaging or even a breaking experience. Such experience, damaging or otherwise, does not take place in isolation. It takes place within a social context. This social context and the relationships of power and influence within it are among the matters explored in the next chapter.

Notes

1 For schema, see Derry (1996), Mandler (1984) and Marshall (1995).

2 A central part in language acquisition, and the development of associated cognitive schema, is understanding of intention in other, particularly human, agents. Tomasello (2001) reviews a range of research which established this as a valuable integrating hypothesis. His clear view from this is that: there are two cognitive foundations for language acquisition: (1) children's growing ability to conceptualise the world in something like the same way as adults and (2) children's growing ability to understand adults' communicative intentions towards particular aspects of that world in particular communicative circumstances (p. 155).

3 Aronson (1980) sees dissonance between events and our preferred schema as being generally resolved through self-deception. Our basic postulate, in this view, is that we see ourselves as beneficent and effective and tend to distort evidence to the contrary to fit with that self-image. Bias is not simply a characteristic of those with least knowledge. 'Experts' can be among the most biased, bringing preset frames of reference to new situations (Evans, 1989). In a work context, 'groupthink' (Janis, 1972) can ensure that individuals seldom question their basic assumptions about a situation since these are reinforced by all the other people around them.

4 In fact Barker went on to lead another school where he recovered his original enthusiasm.

Chapter 3

THE SOCIAL AND POLITICAL CONTEXT OF SCHOOLS

The second key theme of research studies is the complexity of the social and political contexts in which schools are nested. Schools are complicated institutions with multiple goals and complex decision making processes and political influences. This theme aids our understanding of dilemmas in a number of ways:

- In most countries, education is a significant concern of government at national and local levels; the educational policies of governments have profound effects on schools, effects which may be inconsistent and unintended.
- At the level of the individual school, complexity and diversity in the school community can create micropolitical tensions and conflicts.
- Both at national and local level, it is challenging to realise in practice the principles of democratic schooling, even if these could be agreed; they must certainly include a commitment to use democratic means to resolve differences and conflicts, such as those which are characteristic of dilemmas.
- Complexity and tension result from social as well as political change – schools exist in a globalising social context where constant restless change influences purpose and direction in schooling.
- School communities in democratic societies function best when individuals 'trust' each other, but given political divisions, hierarchical organisational structures and a restless social context, building trust can be very challenging.

Political influences on schooling

At the macro-political level in most societies, government (either national or local or more usually a combination of both) is centrally involved in educational policy and associated resourcing. However, governments sometimes aim for ends which may conflict with each other, while the legal framework

Vignette 4

A headteacher has to deal with a young man aged 14 who repeatedly misbehaves in the classroom. The headteacher knows that this young man spends most weekends helping out on his uncle's farm where his physical energy and skills with animals and equipment give him a self-reinforcing positive learning experience. The headteacher also believes that it is in the best interests of this young man to leave school and 'learn through doing' in the world outwith school. The law does not permit extended 'work experience', and curriculum guidance requires that the boy continues to study a range of general education courses (English, Maths and so on) in school. The parents ask the headteacher to connive with them in allowing the boy to work on his uncle's farm for the next eighteen months until he reaches school leaving age. However, a recent conversation with the director of education confirmed that the headteacher must stick to local authority guidelines. She stated quite clearly, 'If any child was injured, or even worse abducted, because we had allowed work experience which had not been properly risk assessed and insured, we would be liable and responsible.' However, when sitting facing the boy and his parents, the headteacher is tempted to connive with the parents and the uncle at a different solution and wonders what advice he might best give the parents.

The headteacher's judgement is that it would be in the boy's best interests educationally to work on his uncle's farm, rather than constantly getting into negative learning encounters in school, encounters which reinforce the boy's self-image as someone who cannot learn. However, the instructions of national and local policy on the management of work experience are quite clear, and the principles on which they are based (equal access to learning and safe risk management) are unarguable. National policy makers are concerned with generalities. They do not have to meet individuals for whom the situation is more complicated.

within which school-based education takes place can be confusing. Vignette 4 illustrates how it is at the level of the individual that these contradictions and tensions become evident.

The framework of law surrounding this vignette is complex. The Standards in Scotland's Schools etc Act (SEED, 2000a) provides that the voice of the student should play an increasingly important role in decisions about their education in accordance with their level of maturity. However, the local authority could be held accountable for any failure if the child (under 16) were to be injured during a work placement, while the headteacher will be held accountable if the child fails to learn at school, achieves little in their terminal school examinations and disrupts the learning of others in his classes.

More generally than this individual case, the 2000 Act establishes that a number of voices must be heard in setting school priorities. In addition to the policies of the local authority (which has statutory responsibility for operating schools), and the overall strategic and legal context set nationally, headteachers must also take account of the views of staff, parents and pupils of the school in setting priorities. While in the statute book, this looks like highly worthy version of consensual democracy at work, in the reality of the school, life is more complex. What happens when, as in Vignette 1 (see Chapter 1), parents and pupils disagree with national guidance, while the local authority puts out one set of advice (encourage healthy eating) but takes contrary action (issuing licences for burger vans to trade outside the school)? Who makes the decision as to what should happen? Who has the power? Who has the influence? Different specialist policy makers deal with their own little bit of policy. The inconsistencies only come together at the level of the school. Many dilemmas can be understood as individual and personalised instances of these inherent tensions within the schooling system. The headteacher who wants to 'blow the whistle' to let the public take part in the debate on resources (Vignette 2 in Chapter 1) represents, in an individual case, a tension between the headteacher's need for an open relationship with her school community and the employee who is not allowed to speak on policy matters. Such legal complexities reflect the different demands and expectations the community has of schools and the pressures which result.

In determining the scale and intensity of these tensions and paradoxes, two headteacher colleagues and I put together a list of tensions and paradoxes (Table 3.1 below). These paradoxes operate as fault lines through school communities. How can a compulsory system be empowering? How can a school system value all young people equally when the only nationally sanctioned public measurement of their achievements ranks them on a linear scale (national examinations at age 16)? The table highlights the contrary forces which can result from these inbuilt tensions in our plural schools, experienced by the headteacher in individual situations as dilemmas.

Often the headteacher is the pivot around which these competing pressures flow. A good example is the use of disciplinary power – a strong expectation of headteachers in schools in the United Kingdom. A primary aim of the Scottish school community is to include all young people, to cultivate in them the habits and dispositions which will allow them to become 'successful learners, responsible citizens, active contributors and confident individuals' (SEED, nd). Yet the use of disciplinary power can foster the development of relationships of antipathy and generate powerful emotions within the individual which act against the ambitions of the school to include and support.

In taking disciplinary actions (whether against staff or against pupils) the headteacher may break down the bonds of trust which are an essential lubricant of school life. Such tensions around school discipline mirror a general confusion in the UK about how we should respond to crimes.

Table 3.1 Paradoxes and tensions of contemporary Scottish schooling

On the one hand ... *but* ...	on the other hand
Multiple intelligencies require different types of learning opportunity	Formal language-based learning is more important than any other kind
Schools should be comprehensive in intake	Parents should be able to choose where to send their child to school
Schools must be regulated by and accountable to the elected council	School communities should be able to make decisions for themselves
Teachers are the experts in education	Teachers need re-educating to understand how education and schooling must change
Schools have never been better (evidenced in parental questionnaires)	Schools have never needed to change more radically or quickly (political manifestos)
Schools should induct young people into broad prosocial values	Schools are agents of an overly influential state and must not push unwelcome and inappropriate values onto local communities
Above all, schools should 'care'	Above all, schools should be efficient
An ideal vision of what school can provide creates a rhetoric of expectation	Resource constraints limit options for delivering the ideal
Rights of children to have their needs met	Rights of staff to fair employment and limited, not limitless, expectation of their work
Equality of opportunity / level playing field	Different starting-points (financial/ academic) allow differential access to opportunity
Curriculum based on individual need	Curriculum based on national guidance
Education as empowerment	Education as socialisation
Ownership of learning by the learner	Compulsory attendance
Comparison of schools by measurable outcome	No comparison of schools by measurable input
Headteachers and staff are held accountable for all aspects of school outcomes	Headteachers and staff have limited responsibility for many of the key determinants of school outcomes
Inclusion of all the community's children is the primary aim	The academic profile of the school and its average attainment is the key priority
We value a broad set of educational aims for our schools, beyond narrow academic performance	The media examine and compare our schools on the basis of the examination results of their pupils
Good schools involve and empower the communities they serve	How this is to be done will be decided nationally, not locally
Schools should include all young people in the community	Schools should exclude those whose behaviour poses a threat to the wellbeing of others
Offences against others in the school community are sources of learning and rehabilitation	Offences against others in the school community require punishment
Education is a public good provided by the state	Education is a private matter for individual parents

Garland (2001) argues that we have moved in Britain from a system of penal welfare to one in which penal policy is emotional not rational, political not professional and retributive and expressive, not rehabilitative. In the microsocial context of the school community, the different individuals involved in disciplinary situations – victim and perpetrator, staff and pupil, discipliner and disciplinee – find themselves at all points on this spectrum and often disagreeing strongly not just with the specifics of how action has been taken in their own situation, but more generally about the principles of justice and fairness that should apply. In the middle is the school headteacher, expected, in the case of individual 'crimes' in school, such as the assault by one pupil of another, to be security officer, investigating officer, prosecution counsel and judge . . . and then to develop a warm and supportive relationship with both the victim and the perpetrator which allows both to be fully functioning members of the school community (Vignette 3 in Chapter 2 illustrates some of the difficulties of such situations). The legal responsibilities of the headteacher in disciplinary policy compete with the professional responsibilities as a trusted educator.

In contrast to the contradictions illustrated so far, some political influences are much clearer and more direct in their intention. Internationally, a strong and recurring feature of much recent discussion of the politics of schooling has been the attention given to the liberal agenda which in the 1980s and 1990s swept through the English-speaking world (Billot, 2003; Fullan, 2003). Key features included:

- more responsibility at school level for operational management;
- less responsibility at school level for policy, seen in the development of a nationally framed curriculum;
- greater accountability at the level of the institution through 'hard' indicators of school performance, such as examination result 'league tables';
- marketisation of the system, through increased parental choice, based on such measures.

The overall approach, consistent with other aspects of New Public Management (Gronn, 2003; Hood, 1991), was to value in professional practice the efficiency and effectiveness with which politically specified goals were achieved. Applied to public welfare policy, this resulted in a combination of 'more choice, more efficiency and more individual responsibility {for implementation}: apparently a winning trinity of ideas' (Hutton, 1995). The educational literature, however, shows that many headteachers experienced great professional tension, from the conflict between this emphasis on 'efficiency' and 'effectiveness' and their professional ambitions to take a wider view of the purposes of schooling. Many of the most powerful and morale sapping dilemmas experienced by headteachers were directly related to reforms of the education system as a whole and resultant tensions and disagreements illustrated in the studies below. Even in the welfare-focused political culture of the Scandinavian countries, school leaders are beginning to experience these tensions and dilemmas (Moos and Moller, 2003). Markets are seen by some as reducing dilemmas. Choice and diversity in the market-place removes the dilemma from the professional. His or her responsibility is to provide a clear and efficient service. If the customer does not like it he or she can 'shop elsewhere'. On the other hand, it is clear that markets can place ethical pressure on professionals to 'hide' or 'mask' tensions in the interests of slick presentation – the studies of Bottery (1998) and Grace (2002) give ample evidence of just these dilemmas in the professional lives of individual school leaders in England. If there are significant and necessary difficulties between what we require from our schools and what they are able to deliver, the market model may not therefore encourage either clear choice or proper civic debate. Instead, political fudging may be concealed beneath a gleaming veneer which masks the tension. In this kind of situation, where tension cannot be acknowledged or debated, the dilemmas facing the professional decision maker may increase as the inherent tensions and conflicts of the situation are suppressed, buried underground, leading to the kinds of emotional pressures outlined in the previous chapter.

The impact of marketising school system reform was the focus of the account by Wildy and Louden (2000) of the dilemmas faced by principals in a large Australian school system. Three essential dilemmas were which permeated all difficult decision making situations within the school (Table 3.2).

Table 3.2 Dilemmas in school restructuring *(after Wildy and Louden, 2000)*

Dilemma	Issues involved		
1. autonomy	*Strong leadership*	*vs*	*Shared leadership*
2. accountability	*External accountability*	*vs*	*Local decisions*
3. efficiency	*Efficient time use*	*vs*	*Collaborative decisions*

The Canadian principals studied by Lam (1996) were facing what he describes as two contrary demands. One was to provide educational equality for all students while also demanding academic excellence as measured by international comparisons and the second involved increasing expectations from declining resources (p. 127). This gap between expectation and resources is a constant theme of studies of headteacher workload (Billot, 2003; Cranston et al., 2003; Murphy, 2003) and of the regular press reports of headteacher stress. Politicians may require a particular end without necessarily providing the means.

Mahony *et al.* (1998) address many of these issues, where the power within a school meets the power which frames the school context, in their discussion 'Who really runs the school?' They find that although there are additional pressures on heads in the new models of power and accountability, there are also opportunities:

> although the policy context at the macro level may shape the parameters of how schools operate, it is at the micro level of the school itself that policy is translated into practice. The head is undoubtedly a highly significant person in this process and may use or misuse her or his considerable power in pursuit of particular values . . . (p. 123)

Headteachers therefore need to have both a clear understanding of the macropolitical context and highly developed micropolitical skills.

Micropolitics inside school communities

The vignettes found throughout this book well illustrate how powerful forces within the school surge around the headteacher. Blase and Anderson (1995) describe three possible routes for the exercise of power by the headteacher: 'power over, power through and power with'. They express a clearly argued preference for 'power with'. However, 'power with' one of the protagonists in each dilemma may be 'power over' another. It is, in part, the consequences of exercising power which 'dilemma-bound' headteachers fear. It is not only headteachers who have power in school communities and the exercise of headteacher power can stimulate the use of power by others, sometimes with destructive effects.

Moller (1996) uses Blase and Anderson to give a characteristically insightful account of the micropolitics of dilemmas, situated within a macropolitical frame. She identifies dilemmas as fundamentally concerned with 'steering' (who is in control and how are they controlling?) and loyalty (to whom, or to what, should I show loyalty in a conflict?). Examples might therefore involve both loyalty and steering. Different forces of authority or power within school communities are in constant dialectical interplay. Power does not all flow from a 'head' through a straightforward hierarchy. Teachers and others within the school community also have power. Headteachers often, surprisingly, perceive themselves as powerless, trapped by a number of competing forces. Although Moller paints a multidimensional picture, in which each dilemma opens out onto a further one and the power to resolve these dilemmas does not rest solely with the headteacher, nonetheless this does not remove, she says, the necessity and responsibility for the headteacher to act – and generally this micropolitical action is a skill headteachers value in their own work.

Duignan and Collins (2003) make similar reports of micropolitical complexity. School principals in their study are seen as constantly evaluating the overall micropolitical consequences of a particular action. What are the potential costs and benefits? What other forces and powers might be generated by the exercise of power by the principal? A typical report involved a school principal who decided to avoid the confrontation with a teacher but believed this was the right decision:

> I have worked in the public sector for many years and I have seen and experienced time, money and emotions spent on people and projects with absolutely no progress or outcomes . . . I have used the time I have 'saved' in this case to foster innovations and work with people who are committed and wish to be involved and do a good job . . . (p. 285)

Knowledge of the micropolitics, the power of the teacher unions, the influence of the staffroom and so on, led this principal to take a hard look at the opportunity cost of taking the case on, and to let it go. Teacher unions, parent advocates, powerful teenage role models – many people in a school community have power. Others outside the school have 'power over' the headteacher and this can also have significant effects. Cowie (2001), for example, in his study of headteachers within a particular Scottish authority found strong echoes of the 'steering' dilemma identified by Moller. He discovered that the biggest source of stress for this group of Scottish headteachers was the strong bureaucratically framed quality assurance requirements of their local authority, which sought managerial compliance, often leading, in the eyes of the headteachers, to professional denial. This was a change to the previous relationship and was a direct result of nationally mandated requirements in the development of quality assurance systems. Simplistic judgements were being made within the new quality assurance framework with consequently negative effects on the feelings that these headteachers had about their work:

> Pressure for control has led to a mechanistic form of quality assurance that contradicts the rhetoric of devolved management, and does not take account of the multiple accountabilities of headteachers . . . that data suggests that established approaches to the governance of secondary schooling are unproductive and dysfunctional . . . [and] that headteachers feel isolated and in danger of being overwhelmed by the changes and pressures of recent years . . . (Cowie, 2001, p. 18)

He goes on:

> The psychological contract between headteachers and the education authority is breaking down . . . [this] . . . is likely to generate low levels of motivation, which, accompanied by changes in the role of

the headteacher, is likely to add to the stresses of headship, contribute further towards feelings of powerlessness, and 'principal burnout', characterised by emotional exhaustion, frustration, depersonalisation and feelings of low personal accomplishment.

Such emotional features of the job, as already seen in the work of Beatty (2000a), have substantial effects on performance and capacity. These micropolitical pressures are exaggerated where there is intense pressure for change. Gronn (2003) sums this up well:

> Organisational transitions are anxiety-inducing because they threaten existing identities, loyalties and commitments . . . In circumstances of institutional transition and identity change, leaders may find themselves to be objects of fantasies of love or hate, and hope or despair . . . psychodynamic theorists have provided powerful explanations of how and why organisation members devise elaborate patterns of defensive and resistant emotional behaviour . . . procrastination, and equivocation, denial of reality and avoidance . . . stalling, buck-passing, playing safe, misrepresentation, fabrication . . . may be developed into calculated micro-political strategies designed to protect key interests . . . (pp. 133–4)

Democratic schooling

Moller (2002) quotes Apple and Beane (1999) in defining the essential conditions for democratic schooling, paraphrased below:

- an open flow of ideas;
- a belief that collectively and individually we can resolve conflicts and problems in fair and non-violent ways;
- critical analysis of policies and practices;
- concern for the welfare of others;
- concern for the dignity and rights of individuals and minority groups;
- an understanding that democracy is not just about 'ideals' but about the values by which we live;
- the organisation of schools should promote democratic ways of living.

This mixture of values and organisational recommendations provides a reasonable starting-point for considering democratic schooling. However, it is not without its difficulties. Democratic ideals such as freedom and equality, for example, often compete. Where there is great individual freedom, inequality increases, while in order to realise equality, freedom has to be restricted. Democratic ways of living require us to balance these competing principles in our institutions, our laws and our lives. There is no perfect democracy. States balance democratic principles in their legal and constitutional systems in different ways. A wide range of historical and situational factors have contributed to different democratic models, with implications for the relative structures and purposes of schooling.

For much of the latter part of the twentieth century, much democratic debate in the United Kingdom has centred on what types of school should exist in a democratic society. The various advocates of diversity point to the specific requirements of separate religious schooling which inducts its students into a complete way of life, or to the advantages of schools independent of government (albeit normally only accessible to those with sufficient income to pay the fees) and, more recently, to the enhanced sense of pride associated with schools which aim for their own locally defined excellencies.

Greater choice and diversity in the system as a whole may reduce the dilemmas experienced by headteachers in any individual school, as suggested by Lawton (2006). Those participating in religious or independent school communities have made an active choice of school, because of a preference for the tighter, less plural set of values which they represent or allow. The headteacher can assume a greater degree of consensus in relation to some key values. Individuals choose to fit within a pre-ordained order and the headteacher is perhaps more likely to see his or her role as being to administer that order. For example, Johnson *et al.* (2000) found 'no ambivalence in the moral code' which applied in Catholic schools, even across international boundaries. Some dilemmas, however, exist in and are particular to these 'less plural' settings. One of the Catholic heads, for example, in my study of Scottish headteachers confided that some of the most difficult dilemmas he faced were in situations where the prescriptions of the Church in areas such as sex education (which he felt duty bound to honour) sat ill alongside the reality of his pupils' lives (to which he felt duty bound to respond).

In contrast, schools which are open to all the community experience much greater internal value plurality with consequent effects on the teachers' perceptions of their role. In comprehensive schools Hamilton (2002) found considerable cognitive dissonance in how staff and pupils handled the inequalities inherent in pupils having different acacdemic abilities: principles of equality and class setting by 'ability' in subject co-existed uneasily. Such cognitive dissonance could increase tensions. There was much greater consensus, and consequently less cognitive dissonance, in her research subjects in independent schools. There is an 'assumed consensus' which those joining the community choose to 'buy into'; the job of the headteacher is to maintain a stable school culture. Carr and Landon (1998, 1999) found that secondary comprehensive school teachers in non-denominational state schools were reluctant to exert any kind of educational influence on their pupils beyond the safe boundaries of their 'subject', recognising moral formation as a 'no go' area, with no 'right and wrong' answers. In contrast, in independent and/or religious schools there was much greater willingness to engage with a broader educational agenda, including the behaviour and mores of young people in their 'private' as well as their school lives.

Many advocates of comprehensive schools argue that choice in schooling exaggerates social inequality and that comprehensive schooling, by opening up educational opportunity, contributes greatly to building a more democratic society. However, it also could be argued that a system which reduces choice and requires all pupils to attend the same kind of school builds a greater degree of structural tension into each individual school. The social tensions characteristic of social plurality in an increasingly individualising society are found *within* each institution. This increases the likelihood of these tensions expressing themselves in individual situations, at least some of which will be experienced as dilemmas. This may be a cost worth bearing because of other benefits of comprehensive school systems (Croxford, 2001; Paterson, 1997a). Paterson (1997b), from a different perspective, sees the route of some of these necessary tensions within the comprehensive system itself. One of the benefits sought through increasing educational opportunity and access is to increase the scope for individual agency and autonomy. Comprehensive neighbourhood schools, with an inclusive community ethos, make a significant contribution to the individualisation of society by empowering individuals through education. They thus release social forces which place a high value on individual agency, an agency most often expressed through the kinds of choices which a uniform state system denies.

In any democratic system, whatever the school structure might be, school culture across all schools needs to develop a commitment to democratic values and to a culture of learning and enquiry. Moller (2002) states that 'democratic thoughts and attitudes must characterise the relationships between those who have their work in schools and the relationship between the school and the local community', but 'schools have been rather undemocratic institutions throughout history'. This is as true of the role of the headteacher as it is of any other part of the school (Johansson, 2004a, 2004b). Riley (2002) examines one aspect of this tension, Mulford (2004) another. If school principals are expected to play a part in developing the democratic understandings of their students, why are they not allowed to share publicly in the political debate about many aspects of policy? This clearly has relevance to Vignette 2 in Chapter 1.

Moreover, the principles on which school as a community of enquiry should be based (see for example Senge *et al.*, 2000) are not by any means agreed. The tension listed above between empowerment and control, or the tension in curriculum design between the expertise of the past and the skills of the future (see for example Moore and Young, 2001), make 'group learning' of the type that produces a clearly defined learning culture (Schein, 1985) difficult. Vignette 5 in Chapter 4 illustrates clearly the difficulties caused in a school by different beliefs about learning. Conflicting views of what democratic schooling should do, and conflicting views of the learning culture appropriate to schooling, increase the complexity and scope of the headteacher's task and the likelihood of difficult dilemmas arising.

However, it is not only the headteacher who has responsibility for resolving dilemmas. Part of democratic living is about coming to terms with difference, and finding ways to resolve our differences peacefully. This way of thinking about democratic schooling reminds us of its collective, community character. The school needs to develop its democratic spaces (meetings, papers, discussions) and the range of techniques of decision making individuals can use in dilemma type situations: mediation and conflict resolution, principled negotiation, inclusive problem solving, ethical analysis. Everyone in a school community faces dilemmas.

Should a pupil who feels unfairly treated give in to a bossy teacher – fairness demands protest but to struggle may make things worse? Should a parent complain about the way in which a member of staff has spoken to their child, knowing that the same member of staff is a volunteer coach for the soccer team in which another of their children plays? Should a member of staff speak to their head of department if they have serious concerns about the declining professional standards of a colleague, although that colleague was very supportive when they had difficulties earlier in their career? The frequency of such conflicts (fairness or utility, accountability or self-interest, loyalty to pupils or loyalty to colleagues) does not make them less difficult. Many individuals, on a daily basis, make decisions to bury their own self-interest, sometimes in the interest of the school community as a whole, sometimes in recognition that they have had or will have their 'day', sometimes through a desire to avoid conflict. Pupils may, for example, be willing to accept classroom boredom in some subjects as a price they pay for the excitement and challenge they experience in others. Staff may accept and live with the frustrating constraints of national guidance in relation to the curriculum because they accept that there are benefits to pupils in a nationwide standard. Parents may be prepared to see less individual attention given to their own children in the junior school if they believe that their child will receive more individual attention further up the school.

In a complex micro-community such as a school, different evaluations can be and are made by a wide variety of community members in relation to all the potential options in decision making situations, from apparently restricted issues such as the menu available at lunchtimes to major issues such as whether classes at age 11 will be set by ability or taught in mixed ability groupings. At all times, members of the community adapt to change, accommodate to decisions they were uncomfortable with, lobby to change systems and structures and, in general terms, establish a modus vivendi in order to come to terms with the tensions and paradoxes they experience. In a democratic school community, the formal systems, processes and principles by which the school operates brings such difficult points of decision to the surface when needed. In the daily hurly burly of living together, the members of the community learn what democracy means in practical terms. In coming to terms with dilemmas and their resolution, members of the community develop an enhanced understanding of democratic living.

It can be argued that dilemmas can be much more easily resolved through the application of force (or the threat of force which underpins laws for example). The forceful advocate of a particular solution imposes it on the other parties through the direct exercise of power (either physical or financial or relational). Adversarial politics, with its commitment to 'black and white' portrayal of the issues, encourages such solutions and often has the advantages of clarity and speed. In democratic societies the abuse of power in forceful methods of resolution is contained by protective laws. However, the spectrum moves a long way from the use of physical force through to 'force of personality'. The headteacher has power which can be used forcefully. In Chapter 5, coercive power is used by the headteacher in the 'worked example'. The use, or abuse, of power through varyingly forceful means, and how its abuse is limited or prevented is another important factor in modelling democratic community living.

In a stable unchanging society, the challenges outlined above would be more than sufficient challenges for schooling. However, our society is far from stable, being permanently characterised by rapid and restless change.

Social complexity

Discussion of the rapidity and complexity of change have become truisms of the contemporary school management text. Favourites in most lists (and these do tend to be lists rather than coherent histories) are:

- the internet;
- relativism – in the absence of certainty, individuals make their own choices;
- economic instability and globalisation increase insecurity and reduce individual agency;
- adolescence has changed: extraordinary purchasing power and credit facilities, well-marketed hedonistic subcultures and consumer-based individualism;
- mistrust of the motives and capacities of political leaders and the political system;
- an unpredictable environmental future;
- increasing terrorist threats;

- changes in the nurture of children through changing family patterns.

In this discourse, the job of the leading educationists in a school community is to empower young people to handle an unpredictable future. Learning skills is thus more important than learning content. Since we do not know what the challenges will be, how can we know what knowledge will be relevant, what interpretative framework will be most useful? Better then to be good at 'problem solving', or 'investigating' than to have a fixed set of answers to predictable problems.

Zygmunt Bauman (1993) is one of the most insightful and lyrical of contemporary commentators on this 'post-modern' condition and its problems. First of all, he argues, there is no agency capable of moving the world forward. Before we even get to asking what is to be done, we must realise that there is no one who can do it. This is because we have realised the limitations of politics. Trapped in their localities, our political institutions still endeavour to control and shape the future in an ordered way, as if their agency could have predictable effects. However, power flows across the globe uncontrollably, through consumer choice, through ideologies of difference, through transnational organisations and flows of money and markets. The crude attempts of politicians to shape our future (war against terror, targeted reductions in hospital waiting lists . . .) are, in this view more notable for the unintended consequences which result than the clearly engineered outcomes which left the planners' desks. This is just as true of educational policies.

Second, even if there were some agency powerful enough to bring it about, we no longer have a vision of what the intended social outcome should be. The various rationally ordered alternatives of Marx (imposed equality) and Hayeck (individual agency) are equally unpalatable. Since we neither know what we want, nor what might help us to get there, we experience constant directionless travel.

Third, this constant movement is both individualised and deregulated: individualised, as there is no socially agreed foundation so it is up to each individual to engage in a constant quest for something new and better; deregulated, since there is no agreed basis, other than through the market, for deciding on whether anything new is in fact an improvement. The individualising and individualised world emphasises choice over compromise and individual meaning over social structure.

This combination is seen by Bauman as fatal for long-term consistent social progress. Individuals operate in an insecure social world – the 'hold on the present', from which they could plan their future with confidence, is shaky. Plans are therefore of necessity short-term, flexibility is highly valued, each episode must be ticked off and its value consumed at the time as it may not fit into a longer term pattern. Sources of livelihood, partnerships of love or of common interest, professional or cultural identity, patterns of health and fitness, values worth pursuing and ways of pursuing them – all are under constant challenge and may change many times in a postmodern lifetime. 'In a life ruled by the precept of flexibility – life strategies, plans and desires can be but short-term' (Bauman, 2001, p. 113).

There is a strong line of argument that these social processes which are confusing to the individual are engendering in many citizens of mature democracies a profound pessimism about the possibilities of politics and a retreat into an individualised world, based around personal preference. These broad social trends are represented quite clearly in the declining interest and participation in democratic politics in many developed democracies, including the UK. If establishing a personal identity as an active citizen is hard for those who are full mature participants in the economy and society, how much harder is it for young people to establish the links between their own individual experience and the broad social, cultural and political frames within which it is constructed. They are bombarded by conflicting messages from powerful and sophisticated modern mass media, told they will have seven changes of career within their lifetime, confused by plural value systems, challenged by the vulnerability of the increasingly fragile 'traditional' family life within their community.

On the back of this kind of analysis, communitarians and social conservatives have separately created a powerful set of arguments for creating protected islands from which to resist what they see as the socially corrosive forces of an economically rationalised social order. While they argue for different solutions, neither advocates the model of state welfare characteristic of much of the public policy of the late twentieth century. The state is seen as both incompetent and inappropriate as a source of moral order. Social conservatives seek freedom to allow the construction of islands oftraditional moral order. In schooling, this can be done through a choice-based and diverse public system. Such a system allows those who wish to do so to protect the authority of tradition within their own schools, where the values they hold dear cannot be corroded by the value relativism of the liberal model (see for example Singh, 2000). Meantime humane advocates of schooling as community formation such as Sergiovanni (1994) accept a degree of plurality and look for the school communities to be built on relationships of trust, mutual concern and shared values of democratic decision making.

Trust

Many recent studies have shown a renewed interest in the concept of trust applied to schooling in particular, and social formation more generally, for example Tschannen-Moran and Hoy (1997), Bottery (2003), Forsyth et al.

(2006), Hoy and Kupersmith (1984). Bryk and Schneider (2002), in one of the fullest and most convincing studies, make a case that 'trust' is a fundamental glue, holding school communities together and explaining much of the variance between schools. They identify three types of trust in human communities:

- organic trust: this occurs in communities where everyone shares a set of values and expectations about behaviour that requires no explanation or justification; it is typically found in rural / premodern societies and groups;
- contractual trust: this type of trust is characteristic of much of modern life; it exists as an underpinning framework of legal obligation, ensuring that those you are dealing with keep their word, and do what they said they would do;
- relational: trust between people based on a shared personal relationship and shared expectations developed from that relationship.

Their longitudinal research in the City of Chicago education system showed that those schools which were rich in relational trust succeeded best in meeting the challenges of contemporary schooling. Such trust needed to exist between all the key stakeholders. In a relationship of trust, dilemmas are approached together, with a recognition of the positive intentions of those involved, an intention to work together to overcome any difficulties and to continue to move forward together. The importance of 'intention' echoes the work of cognitive psychologists who link emotion, cogntion, language and relationships.

Bryk's school-based enquiries find echoes in Rothstein's broader enquiry (2003) into different patterns of democratic association and expectation in different states. Social trust, Rothstein argues, is accumulated through efficiency and fairness in the operations of the institutions of government. If you cannot trust institutions of government, then you cannot trust other people within your society, with devastating effects on social institutions and standards of behaviour in public life, as seen in many different states of the world. Where bureaucratic process and professional codes of ethics and practice ensure fair treatment, people will accept outcomes, even where these go against them. Where process is seen to be biased or unfair or self-interested, individuals may justify to themselves the use of any means to secure their own advantage, thus causing further disadvantage to the whole system. If, for example, you live in a society where the courts and the police are reasonably impartial and effective in how they handle cheaters (those who use inappropriate means to obtain personal ends or break contracts or steal or commit violent acts . . .), then social trust will increase. You, and others, will generally believe that people in your society will be more inclined to make socially positive collaborative and trusting choices, since they know that is how most others will behave and that there is both an effective external process and an internalised normative stigma involved in detecting and eliminating untrustworthy behaviour. There is a constant need to balance and rebalance the relationship between a public institution and those whom it is designed to serve, and to maintain the ethical integrity of public service, free from financial or political influences. A recent UK survey of public attitudes (Hayward *et al*., 2004) demonstrates high levels of public trust in headteachers, among other front line professionals and identifies some clear principles for conduct in public life designed to generate trust.

Taking this model into schooling, a new kind of relationship is created between state and schools: the relational complexity of the modern school provides an organic analysis of how public welfare services are delivered. In this account, a simplistic hierarchical model of accountability and control, with politicians setting the political compass and professionals charged with responsibility for bureaucratic implementation, is replaced by a more complex model in which power and influence operate at all levels. Paterson (1997b) argues that 'imposed bureacratic reform' has, in any event, been shown not to work. State legislated social engineering, in education as in other policy areas, is now seen as ineffective. It simply cannot work well enough given the complexity and essential unpredictability of the social world it seeks to order. Its failure forces a new model on our politics. In this less determinate environment of change, knowledge of what to do and what might work is produced by individuals interacting with each other, creating their own agendas. A foundational tension in this new democratic order is that one must first acknowledge the autonomy of others if one is to work with them to influence the direction and experience of social order. In this way of looking at education, schools are not simply there to equip individuals to make choices and find their way through a meaningless individualised social maze. They generate and store social trust and social capital (Coleman, 1988; Bryk and Schneider, 2002) for the community as a whole through shared experiences and shared values. A school is the first place where a citizen learns whether or not they can trust the community in which they live.

However, there are also difficulties with a state funded public education system occupying a moral space; there are dangers in the imposition of a publicly sanctioned 'social morality'. Discussion of values, often competing values, within ethical rather than political frames of reference may offer a more secure basis within which to analyse the purposes of schooling. Such reflection is the theme of the next chapter.

Chapter 4

ETHICAL PERSPECTIVES

Dilemmas often stimulate ethical enquiries: is there a right or wrong response to a particular situation?; are there shared values or principles among those involved which can be used to shape discussion towards agreement?; can we agree on what might be desirable or undesirable consequences? These kinds of questions, systematically or accidentally, require discussion of values and their application. Some of the values held by individuals within a school community are in conflict with each other and may also be in competition with the espoused values of the school. Moral enquiry aims to establish a basis for adopting particular values beyond a simple individual preference. Ethical practice applies such values to specific situations. In this chapter, our understanding of dilemmas is further enriched through four ethical perspectives:

- Ethical issues are often involved in the dilemmas headteachers face.
- Ethical principles often need to be held in balance, not forced to compete.
- Ethical judgement in situations of moral complexity can only be made in the situation, not in general; those best placed to make such judgements have cultivated virtues such as wisdom and integrity.
- Dialectical thinking captures the tensions and uncertainties of these matters better than linear positivism.

Ethical issues are often involved in the dilemmas headteachers face

Many research studies such as those of Begley (1999b) and Roche (1999) use ethical interpretation to deliver real understanding of what is at stake for headteachers in the dilemmas they describe. Headteachers themselves used ethical concepts frequently in the research studies. Dempster and Mahony (1998) found 'concern with ethical issues was always at a practical level, raised by example rather than by the domains from which most ethical issues originate' (p. 126). Some of the key values at stake for headteachers in particular situations were isolated, including 'multiculturalism, equity, social justice, empathy, accessibility, intellectual humility'. In my research with Scottish headteachers (Murphy, 2002), there were strong ethical concerns. In discussion, these headteachers often asserted the primary importance of 'the child at the centre' of every dilemma. One respondent stated that politics could get in the way of the child. 'Usually', she said, 'there is some reason for disagreement underneath the "politics" of the situation . . . the head has to go past the politics to get to these underlying and very specific factors'.

One of the most common dilemmas in encountered by Duignan and Collins (2001) was 'care' vs 'rules'. Some Australian school principals argued strongly that strictly following the rules disadvantaged some individuals. Rules offered guidance but individual decisions always had to be made. Others believed that the best protection for all was in consistency within the rules. For example, a school principal is quoted as having allowed a student, who had been disciplined, to participate in a major athletic activity (p. 289) even though the rules prohibited this. She thus put the principle of care (giving attention to the needs of the individual) over the principle of rules (ensuring consistent treatment for everyone who behaves in a certain way). In two other examples, however, school principals regretted placing care above rules. The rules, by being bent, had been weakened. They later 'believed [that] care-based choices were not the wise course of action for themselves. They should have followed the rules and would do so in future' (p. 20). Yet had they kept to the rules, surely they would have been left with regret at the damage to the individual students involved. This is the very nature of dilemma.

It was common for headteachers in this research group to refer directly to their own values as a source of support in helping them resolve these situations, but that they found this difficult. Headteachers are said to struggle with 'normative complexity' (the fact that people have different views about what a good life involves) and with competing views about their own role and position and about the purposes of schooling. Where these increasingly contested issues were to be resolved at school level, the headteacher felt cast into the role of sole moral arbiter:

> In their discussions with us, heads reported that they often felt alone, cast in the role of arbiter or mediator relying on personal values and professional ethics to find a morally defensible solution (Duignan and Collins, 2001, p. 132)

Ehrich *et al.* (2006) found that care for the welfare of individual students emerged as a high priority for the headteachers, while tensions over underperforming members of staff, or arising from conflict between professional values and external directives were also prominent. Another strong feature was a perceived tension between the needs of the individual and the needs of the community as a whole. Heads themselves clearly varied greatly in how they understood and interpreted the values involved and often seem not to have the concepts or ideas with which to interpret them. Dempster and Berry (2003) in another very full Australian study, later reinforced (Dempster *et al.*, 2004), categorise dilemmas as essentially ethical in character, but headteachers as ill equipped to deal with them. They describe headteachers as 'blindfolded in a minefield'. Their 'professional' values, derived from their experience, did not equip them for the more complex ethical considerations they now faced.

Moller (1996) links the micropolitical and ethical perspectives. Principals have a view of what might be right or wrong in the situations involved but do not regard it as appropriate to allow such considerations to interfere with what is essentially an institutional situation in which organisational values and micropolitical considerations must prevail. 'Morality' is temporarily 'suspended' by school principals. Moller takes this notion of 'suspended morality' from the work of Campbell (Campbell, 1992), who argues that headteachers in particular, and teachers in general, lack a sufficiently clear ethical compass.

In her award-winning doctoral study of how teachers and principals cope with conflicting values, *Personal Morals and Organisational Stress* (1992), Campbell explored critically, using the models provided by organisational theory (e.g. Ashbaugh and Kasten, 1984), how teachers and school principals viewed potential conflicts between personal values and group or organisational imperatives. Individuals develop various 'techniques' which allow them to suspend personal morality temporarily while 'at work'. They can then occupy a middle ground, somewhere between continuous commitment to the organisation and outright conflict with the organisation. Techniques used include false necessity ('I have no choice'), self-deception ('if I don't acknowledge the situation I won't have to confront it') and situational adjustment ('I'll accommodate to what is easiest in the situation, for example silence or unenthusiastic compliance'). In situations where there is a very strong group framing of the experience, demanding high levels of loyalty to the group (e.g. to a school or to the union), 'covert subversion' or 'furtive disobedience' (Rich, 1984) may be used as conflict avoidance strategies and 'whistle blowers' who oppose the group may attract the highest opprobrium.

Campbell interviewed teachers and principals about real value conflicts they had experienced and also presented vignettes, similar to those in this book, demanding a judgement, for example:

- The principal is asked to write a reference for a student who exhibits anti-social behaviour, knowing that not getting the job will aggravate the child's behaviour.

- A teacher sees a male colleague offer a 12-year-old female student a lift and feels uncomfortable.

Campbell was particularly interested in how and when the interviewees would feel moved to 'take a stand'. Teachers were disinclined to do so where this might cause personal inconvenience or problems with colleagues. In examining the responses of school principals, Campbell was astonished that 7/10 reported that they had not experienced value conflicts personally in their role. They did not conceptualise the issues raised in the vignettes as being moral or ethical, but saw them as practical issues to be resolved in such a way as to 'keep everyone happy'. Trying to achieve a consensus, or assessing the likely consequences and avoiding confrontations which might result were favoured strategies. Although many of the responses included a reference to 'doing the best for the child', Campbell observed that this seemed to get lost before the final decision was made. It was a rhetorical rather than a practical commitment. Campbell argued that this apparent lack of concern for ethical concepts such as 'truth, justice and fairness' was very worrying. Conflicts were often seen as 'problems for other people', with the role of the principal being mediation. She concluded that the morality of the school is thus defined as relativist (each person constructs his or her own morality) and emotivist (moral behaviour is a matter of personal preference). Campbell's analysis sees teachers and principals as individuals lost in big institutions (the state school) where 'ethical foundations have been replaced by bureaucratic imperatives and role expectations' (Campbell, 1992, p. 452). The key role of school and professional peer culture in determining principals' and teachers' response is a strong theme in this study. Campbell has since built a strong body of work arguing that ethical frames of reference need much greater prominence within the teaching profession generally and among headteachers in particular (Campbell, 1996; 2000 and 2003). If headteachers do not typically use well founded understandings of ethical principles to inform their practice, but are instead cast adrift amid a see of competing micropolitical forces, this is professionally and educationally unacceptable and needs to be addressed.

   Can ethical principles help the headteacher in Vignette 5? The politics of this situation, which may give considerable power to the teacher involved, led the headteacher to conclude that the 'best interest of the children' might be best served by supporting the teacher and avoiding a debilitating conflict among the staff. By conceding on her own educational values, the headteacher hopes to avoid a deeper value conflict with potentially worse effects, but she reckoned without the political power of the pupils involved. Ethics has become politics. Ethical principles, as Campbell has suggested, seem to take a back seat. Systematic examination of this territory is clearly needed.

Vignette 5
A new headteacher has convinced most of the staff of the school to sign up to a positive policy supporting good behaviour through rewards. Teaching staff are to attempt, in general, to issue two positive referrals (letters home praising pupils) for every disciplinary sanction so that the tone of the class is one of 'looking for the positives' rather than 'reacting to negatives'. An older member of staff, who is a successful teacher, has resisted the policy, stating that 'They should not be rewarded for what we expect them to do anyway.' The headteacher has not pushed the issue as the teacher is popular and influential in the staffroom and, if alienated, could cause real splits among the staff. In addition, she will retire in 2 years, having given over 30 years outstanding service to the school and its community, and the headteacher feels that she should show respect for this teacher by not creating a situation of potentially bitter conflict near the end of the teacher's career. At the Student Council, the issue of consistency in the new policy is raised. One 10-year-old girl, who is in this teacher's class, is very incensed. She complains that her peers see the whole policy as very unfair because only some teachers take it seriously and others do not. The headteacher feels that the pupils are pushing her into a course of action she would rather not take.

Her professional instincts tell her she should go with the students. She knows that if she does not she may lose her credibility as an effective leader. On the other hand, she does not want to become embroiled in a long-running conflict with the member of staff. Teachers have strong legal and contractual protections and a strong collegial loyalty. Their view of 'professional discretion in the classroom' may be quite different from the headteacher's. Strong personalities in the staffroom can influence staff morale and teamwork. In deciding not to take this teacher on, the headteacher had reckoned that the overall impact on the school of a conflict would be worse than the inconsistency that she now has tolerated, but she now had to face another conflict.

Ethical principles often need to be held in balance, not to compete

Ethical principles may seem to confuse rather than to clarify a dilemma. Even those to which most people subscribe can compete with each other. Which principle should we choose? One person's freedom is another's inequality (Vignette 4). One person's justice is another person's injustice (Vignette 3). Should this be a matter of personal preference, for each person to decide? Common-sense expressions such as 'we are all entitled to our point of view' suggest a fundamentally 'emotivist' philosophy, in which the fact that your feel your view is the right one is sufficient to justify it. Discussion is useless, as respect for difference is more important than any collective endeavour to seek the truth or to try to agree what is right in a particular situation. The philosophical tradition of moral enquiry is, nonetheless, such a collective endeavour and there now follows a brief overview of some contributions which shed some further light.

Alasdair MacIntyre (1981), one of the foremost contemporary moral philosophers, criticises the 'emotivism' which he says has become the normative morality of our age. People, he says, take refuge in emotivism as a way of responding to life in a plural society, in which a primary requirement is tolerance and respect for difference. However, even if we wanted to try to reach agreement, we could not, since we are always arguing from different premises or within different ways of constructing the moral world. Since we have no common rational basis on which to conduct arguments, when these affect action we require to engage in conflict resolution based on bargaining. This produces an expedient morality in which the best that can be hoped for is to resolve conflict through trading interests, not by seeking the truth collectively. This kind of bargaining is founded on an ethics of utility, where others are seen as means not ends. There is thus a moral vacuum at the heart of our social experience. On the one hand, in the modern age we accept that reason cannot describe the essential characteristics of being human towards which behaviour should aim and by which it should be judged. On the other hand, technology has given us the means to do lots of things, without us having to agree whether these are worth doing. Modern living has thus become dominated by a bureaucratic obsession with effectiveness in relation to limited goals in the absence of any real debate about what constitutes our purposes in life. We cannot move forward together in our understanding of these problems because we have no agreed rational basis for discussion.

MacIntyre himself defines human purpose very firmly within a tradition of Western philosophy deriving from Aristotle through Thomas Aquinas to the modern day. In *Whose Justice, Which Rationality?* (1988) and *Three Rival Versions of Moral Enquiry* (1990), he tries to justify his own understanding of human purpose, and thereby show that his moral arguments (based on an ethics of 'virtue') have greater intellectual coherence than other rational traditions. However, Vokey (2001) has criticised MacIntyre's intellectualist bias, arguing that MacIntyre gives special privilege to decentred rational argument and ignores what Vokey calls 'reasons of the heart', the affections and desires of human beings for moral order and goodness. Vokey argues that reason and desire must play complementary roles in defining human goods. For him, MacIntyre's account is insufficiently grounded in the depth and complexity of human experience, particularly contemporary experience of plurality, where an individual may call on several different traditions simultaneously in interpreting and making sense of choices. Vokey builds from Macintyre towards a multidimensional theory of moral behaviour. Our social experiences must be interpreted through more than our intellect. This is not a naïve emotivism which sees feelings as primary, but one which gives them a necessary place in understanding our moral world. It recognises that people are not generally driven to action by abstract moral argument. People change their individual values to fit in with others whom they trust, or for whom they have affection.

Some rational theorists have argued that our understanding of right and wrong in social behaviour derives from our political need to reach agreements, codified in a just legal framework which should govern our relationships. The most impressive of these theories is that of Rawls (1971) who creates an intellectual defence for principles of justice being at the heart of morality. For Rawls, democratic societies are primarily concerned with justice. The construction of a just society involves each person acting as if behind a 'veil of ignorance'. We should act in building our society as though we did not know what position in society (authority, wealth, advantage) we occupy and what therefore the consequences of our actions might be for ourselves as individuals. This 'ethic of justice' continues to be influential. Through it, rationalist attempts to provide a morality based on 'decentred reason', an argument or set of arguments by which every fair minded person would be persuaded, continue into the present day. Headteachers, when using their decision making power would, in this analysis, operate behind a 'veil of ignorance' and would require to examine each decision from the point of view of each person affected.

Postmodern morality balances moral forces differently, prioritising the individual and his or her choices over any system or authority. For the postmodern mind, human beings cannot understand the world they live in. Faced with the overwhelming power of state and technology, *critique* has the highest value in the political and moral world. Traditional community-based moralities, and more recent attempts to build rationally-based moralities by force (universalist projects such as that of Soviet Russia), represent the tyranny of the community over the individual and must be resisted. In a complex plural world each individual participates in many communities. Only his or her own life brings unity to this experience.

Habermas (e.g. 1986) takes up this position of critique, but tries to use it constructively, to create a better balance of social power. For him, industrial processes and bureaucratic organisations dominate the individual, leaving no space for anything other than expressions of individual taste, which cannot change anything. A 'communicative space', a place where right and wrong choices and behaviour can be negotiated without preference or influence being given to those with wealth, tradition or power, must be created to counterbalance the power of industry and bureaucracy. Public discourse in this communicative space should create the terms of social engagement, using the cognitive and moral resources offered by the traditions of disciplined enquiry: traditions which need to be repossessed within the public space, not distorted within overspecialised academic discourses which disempower by introspection. The different perspectives of technology, aesthetics and morality can be taken to extremes and distort our understanding. Habermas argues that we need to balance this potential for extremes by ensuring that each of these perspectives is within the communicative space. Considerable tension can be engendered in school communities by the power of critique. Critique constantly questions the bases on which decisions are made and examines the interests of those making the decisions. Are they really 'in the best interests of the children', or do they perceive these best interests as being 'conformity to the established order' – 'acquiescence in subservience'? Following Habermas, what 'communicative spaces' exist for common meanings to be re-established? Are technology, aesthetics and morality balanced in our debates, or does a technological focus – with its clearer, more limited, short-term measurable objectives – dominate the discussion and determine the values which will count in a contemporary school community?

Feminist literature of the 1980s developed a different perspective on ethical argument, identifying an ethic of care. Gilligan (1982) argued that the prioritisation of function above care, of production above nurture, derives from a Western tradition in which the activities of men have been seen as more valuable than those of women and a rebalancing is needed. The ethic of care attaches a high value to forming and sustaining close relationships. Whatever reason might argue would be the rights and wrongs of an individual situation in the abstract, situations never occur in the abstract, but happen to real people. In the real situation, feelings of concern and relationships of care often balance abstract notions of justice with compassion and connectedness. In arguing that an ethic of care should take first place in educational considerations, Noddings (1992) articulated the values already in operation in many school communities. Within an ethic of care, the legalism of 'disinterested justice' is replaced by 'understanding' and 'support' encouraging trust, commitment and reciprocity. The 'ethic of care' is not a substitute for justice, but restores a proper balance. Caring on its own is seen as insufficient. Although caring facilitates choices which do good, there are many individuals in schools who have an abundance of care but 'whose efforts somehow ended in failure and frustration' (Willower, 1999, p. 129). Willower argues that the argument in favour of care, or justice for that matter, as a primary orientation in evaluating ethical dilemmas is misplaced:

> A more fundamental problem is how to translate caring and good intentions into outcomes that actually benefit others. This is one of the basic concerns of ethical theory, a concern that is stinted by ethical theorists that de-emphasise the processes of making moral choices in concrete situations. (p. 130)

Some authors have attempted to merge these 'competing rationalities' into a conceptual framework which might assist school principals in making decisions. Perhaps the most familiar ethical framework in common use in education is the tripartite frame developed by Starratt (1994, 2003) based on an ethic of justice (e.g. Rawls), an ethic of critique (e.g.Habermas), and an ethic of care (e.g. Noddings). These ethics complement each other, and each is needed in the project of 'building an ethical school'. Starrat thus makes clear that ethics is important not just to help the headteacher make good decisions, but also because it is part of the fundamental purpose of schooling. It may be that the balance between these different ethical models varies according to school and situation. There would, for example, be a strong argument that the ethic of care should take priority in pre-school, special or primary school settings, yet even in these settings, children's sense of 'care' often relates to 'fair treatment', a strong element in the ethic of justice, while critique ensures that the interests of the least powerful take centre stage.

Shapiro and Stefkovich (2001), building on Starrat (and using the case study approach to ethical training found in Strike *et al.*, 1988), elaborate an elegant model. Strike *et al.* had described situations where different worthy principles of practice (involving, for example, intellectual liberty, individual freedom, equality of opportunity, authority and democracy) were in competition in specific situations or dilemmas. In the analysis of the cases, reference is made to different traditions in ethical reasoning and moral philosophy to help tease out some of the complexity, but the process seems to involve a 'pick and mix' approach to these traditions of moral reasoning, without a guiding principle to give a clear direction. Shapiro and Stefkovich go beyond this. They argue that the diversity and complexity of contemporary schooling requires a 'multi-paradigm' model to guide and support choices for action, and that the most significant, and synthesizing, paradigm is the 'ethic of the profession', a dynamic paradigm which includes justice, care and critique. In any specific complex dilemma situation, the headteacher requires to apply the ethic of the profession. They argue that skills and understanding must be developed by the decision maker (in this case the headteacher) and that this can only happen through the kind of dialogue which exposes the headteacher to the different perspectives of care, critique and justice, represented in the specific situation within which the dilemma occurs. Ethical practice then results from deeper ethical understanding, with priority developing around the 'best interests of the child'.

This notion of the 'best interests of the child' is clearly a powerful professional value, emerging, unforced and without reference to any supporting literature, in a number of the phenomenological studies of the experience of headship cited above. However, as Dearden (1968) argued a generation ago, 'interests' is no basis for authoritative judgement, since people will differ in their view of what constitutes a child's best interests. Taking the example of Duignan's poorly behaved athlete, who was allowed to run despite the rules, is it in the child's best interest to learn that by manipulating a powerful decision maker, he or she can overturn the rules, or would it be better for the athlete to learn that social rules are consistent?

Shapiro and Stefkovich describe ethics as a process. Their students may therefore have benefited much more from the *discussion* than from the model. Each individual, they say, must come to their own professional decisions, albeit with reference to the broader ethical canvas they paint. Although it is a sincere attempt to support a better understanding of the ethical issues, and although the students following their programmes have by self report deepened both their understanding and their judgement, many of the key dilemmas arise precisely because there is disagreement about the 'best interests of the child' and so this model only offers weak support. Begley (2004b) places the three 'ethics' in a preferred sequence – first critique (explore the viewpoints), then care (nurture and support), then justice (maximise benefits while protecting rights). But this formula is no better in helping resolve much disagreement. Compulsory curriculum entitlement or individually negotiated curriculum (Vignette 4)? Enforced healthy eating or choice to eat unhealthily (Vignette 1)? Treating individuals with respect or treating issues of community safety with respect (Vignette 6)?

Similar difficulties confront the kinds of ethical reasoning found in general studies of decision making, or many of those focused on other professional fields.[1] Interesting and valuable as these general or comparative treatments are, none of them purport to offer to the headteacher, confronted with a dilemma, a formula which, when applied, would automatically lead to the 'right' or the 'best' decision. Are there any overriding ethical principles, or an ethical code of practice, which can lead the confused headteacher to the right or the best decision? Campbell (2000) draws attention to the limitations of this view. Even were a complete professional code of ethics to be developed (and it is desirable to do this), it could never provide an objective reference point for the kinds of complex specific situations with which school leaders are routinely confronted. Only shared internalised values within a school community can provide such a grounding.

Furman addresses this problem through her identification of a further paradigm, the 'ethic of the community' (Furman, 2004). She defines the ethic of community as a moral responsibility to engage in communal processes which address the moral purposes of schooling and the ongoing challenges of daily life in schools. The ethic of community sees the communal not the individual as the primary locus of moral agency. The assumption underlying the individualist approach to decision making is that individual educators, by applying principles of ethical analysis, can think through ethical dilemmas and make decisions that are ethically sound. But all dilemmas involve people in the community who are not just objects on which a benevolent school leader school leader can act, but people who must be involved in its resolution. The ethic of community captures the centrality of this need for communal processes in a way that the ethics of justice, critique, care and the profession do not. Thus, the ethic of community is a missing link, she argues, in thinking about the relationships between ethics, leadership practice, and the moral purposes of schooling.

Furman's arguments build on other thinkers who emphasise the 'I and We' of ethical living (see for example Etzioni, 1997). A powerful strand of this community-based morality argues for the cultivation of 'virtues' which support individuals in coming to the right decision in complex situations. MacIntyre is among many who espouse an ethics of ''virtue' (MacIntyre, 1981). Statman (1997) and Hursthouse (2001) provide fuller introductions to this perspective. What is ethical in a given situation is 'what a virtuous person would do'. Virtues are cultivated within communities and applied through practical wisdom (an Aristotelian concept). The development of this 'practical wisdom' to assist individuals in making decisions in the face of complex choices and dilemmas is a social responsibility, not just a characteristic of individuals. Such wisdom is best supported within communities which value the social and intellectual habits which encourage wise reflection. Communities must therefore find ways to deal with these dilemmas collectively. Through new contracts of engagement (procedural), through communicative action (occupying a disinterested space), through the negotiation of new moral consensus while recognising that this carries its own dangers, ways to move forward can and should be found. In schools, this would require revisiting, in an atmosphere of trust, respect and care, the differences between individuals in how they conceive of and respond to their social situation and its tensions and responsibilities. Starrat's recent work on the ethical characteristics required of school leaders (Starrat, 2003; 2005) locates the ethical leader within such a community.

A 'community-based' ethics, while a rich concept, still leaves the question in a plural society, 'which community of many?', a perspective reinforced by the further explorations of Shapiro and Stefkovich (2003), who find ethical responses varying from one community to another. Are these decisions to be made at the level of the individual school (each school developing its own processes for deciding how to resolve difficult conflicts of values or interests), or should schools reflect specific communities within society as a whole (for example religious communities), or are there some society-wide considerations that should be foundational, (such as the requirements of democratic schooling outlined above)? These considerations echo the political and social concerns of Chapter 3 above. Ethics of justice, care, critique, community and of virtue all have merit and philosophers may, and often do, discuss in general terms which has priority. This does not help the 'blindfolded' headteacher trying to work out which should take priority in a given situation.

Ethical judgement in situations of moral complexity can only be made in the situation

Absolutist systems of moral thinking (whether reason- or faith-based) may seek to impose judgement through power or authority, but in democratic societies where plurality is accepted there is a commitment to finding the balance through dialogue and mutual understanding. While it makes sense to conduct such discussion at the abstract and general level of 'human society', the theme which emerges most strongly from the overview above is that general principles always need to be applied in specific situations. Situated judgement is needed because of the complexity and individualisation of the social experience (Bauman, 1993). Situated judgement is needed because it develops from and contributes to the local reconstruction of social meaning through dialogue and discussion (Etzioni, 1997). Situated judgement is required because it balances the abstractions of justice with the personal understanding of care (Noddings, 1992). Situated judgement requires the kind of practical wisdom which alone can deal with the indeterminate world of human behaviour, as opposed to the determinate world of making things (Aristotle interpreted for the modern age by Dunne, 1993).

Charles Larmore (1987) agrees with much of the neo-Aristotelian project and offers a complex view of the necessary tensions and complexities of modern moral choice. Judgement is central. Training, experience and the development of moral character all depend on the community structuring its moral life and the educational processes which inform it. The state must be maintained as a neutral territory against the challenges of holistic theories which attempt to capture it. It is the neutrality of the state and the public sphere which allows moral flourishing in other areas. For Larmore, morality is heterogeneous – sources of moral value are varied and judgement often involves situational responses, balancing the different relevant valuations of consequence, duty and partiality. From a different angle Sadurski (1990) also finds neutrality in the law as an important foundation for moral activity.

Varela (1999) connects psychology and cultural anthropology to morality. 'Situatedness' is the capacity to make wise judgements in action based on complex learned interpretative schema, not abstracted rationality. Individuals frame their understanding of a situation and consequent appropriate action using a range of concepts, ideas and relationships. In traditional communities, such 'schema' are uniform across the society, are learned through community living and certain people (usually older) have particular skill in their application (wisdom). The ethical behaviour of the wise is not to do with rigidly following precepts or obeying rules but comes from applying 'extended inclinations'. The challenges of plural living can fragment the self and complexify and fragment the schema.

There is much of direct relevance to schools in this Aristotelian concern with applying practical wisdom through cultivating the virtues which underpin it. Schools are charged in this view with a substantial moral responsibility, to educate future citizens in complex situated judgements, informed by virtuous dispositions cultivated within the community. A shared understanding of this mission is needed if those in the school community are to benefit from it. Where those in the school community see the school as essentially concerned with the transmission of specific skills of value to the individual in making their own choices, such a 'moral community' model of schooling is unlikely to work well.

Dialectical thinking captures the tensions and uncertainties of the dilemmas

Linear rationality with its limited concepts does not reflect the potential of human situations. It substitutes a static 'word' for the real-life ever-changing interactive object, process, event or concept. Closed linear reasoning seeks to resolve tensions in an unreal imagined space, outwith time, where no one makes choices and decisions but only discusses in abstract what is or should be. Dialectical reasoning, by contrast

- holds potential futures in tension against each other, recognising that only the progression of real events in time will lead to resolution and new tensions;
- recognises interdependence – an object, process, event or concept only makes sense because it is dependent and connected;
- acknowledges the incompleteness of words and the propositions constructed from them: the positive expresses what the thing is, but needs to be balanced by a negative weight expressing its potential to be something else (because it is always moving to an indeterminate future);
- links thinking and acting, knowing and known, action and reaction, agent and lifeworld: an epistemological as well as a moral viewpoint, in which the self and the world in which it seeks to act are interdependent.

Hodgkinson (1983), in applying some of the insights gained from ethical understanding to the challenges of leadership, uses dialectical language to capture the dynamic quality of these challenges. For Hodgkinson, leadership is a philosophically-based activity in which the activities of praxis (philosophy-in-action) unite theory and practice. In attempting to understand why people do what they do, Hodgkinson refers to a typology of the values which may apply in deciding on the merits of a particular decision or course of action. The interplay across different types of valuation and motivation can be analysed by philosophy but is also lived out in the decisions made by individuals.

This dialectical tension in ethical decision making is complemented by another tension which exists as a result of the competition between two principles which might govern how we should resolve conflicts of motivation or value. One principle ('the principle of principle') suggests that all decisions should be referred to the higher authority of moral principle (as Campbell sometimes appears to argue). Yet every decision that becomes a matter of such principle places great strain on the emotional resilience or structural character of the relationships involved. Clauser and Gert (1990) provide a convincing critique of this approach in medical ethics, which they call 'principilism', often a 'post hoc' justification of decisions by reference to absolute principles. There can be no room for compromise. It is one thing or another. A competing principle ('the principle of least principle') suggests that all decisions should be referred down the chain to the lowest level at which the matter can be resolved, thus ensuring that what is at stake in a particular conflict does not become an irresolvable conflict. Hodgkinson sees these two principles as being in constant tension – a necessary dialectic of moral complexity at the heart of all decisions. How these tensions are handled will determine the quality and character of an organisation or community. Leadership involves balancing these tensions in practice and is shared throughout an organisation.

In dialectical thinking it is not necessary for one principle to outweigh another. This kind of thinking represents more fully the complex reality of the dilemma where the headteacher often feels that he or she is holding onto tensions that are at the heart of the community and in the best case using them constructively, with creative force, to move to a new place.

Conclusion

Raising the corner of the 'blindfold' has demonstrated further links between the three complementary thematic perspectives which have been the focus of Chapters 2, 3 and 4. Some aspects of the ethical turn out to be political (Nielsen, 1996). It can be argued that plural democracy is itself an ethical theory in which we value each other's differences, and the peaceful resolution through legal process of any tensions which result, more than we value any set of absolute principles in which we believe (Chapter 3). As we grow in our relationships with each other, and our understanding of our differences, we learn new ways of conceptualising what is happening in social situations, and understand the emotions which summarise our feelings about this (Chapter 2). In acting within the educational community, it is not enough for the headteacher to display this understanding, however sophisticated and intellectually coherent. It must also clearly inform their practice and behaviour. Trust is once again seen to be at the heart of these issues. Ethical theory allied to unethical practice (perceived or real) destroys trust. Ethical practice, whether accompanied by theory or not, builds trust. According to Beck and Murphy (1997, p. 33), 'ethics is less about making decisions using objective principles and more about living morally in specific situations'. Ethics thus also involves the character of the individual – their internalisation of the moral values and virtues that guide personal and professional practices, including the resolution of moral dilemmas encountered in daily practice. In this way an ethics of virtue also finds its place as a necessary element in the repertoire of the headteacher.

Does this provide a way forward? Overwhelmed by so much guidance, and by the frequency and range of the dilemmas to be faced, how is the headteacher to make any decisions at all? The next chapter aims to move beyond the 'paralysis of analysis' by describing a toolkit for the headteacher to use.

Note

1 See Thomson (1999) for an excellent primer on critical reasoning in ethics. Kidder (2003) provides an accessible introduction. See also Callahan (ed.) (1988) and Lawrence (1999) for treatments of professional ethics across a range of professions and Rest and Narváez (1994) for work on the moral development of trainee professionals measured by Rest's 'Defining Issues Test'.

Chapter 5

DEALING WITH DILEMMAS:
SOME PRACTICAL GUIDANCE

This penultimate chapter takes the insights offered from the previous chapters, which have opened up to view the nature of the professional dilemmas of headship, and applies them practically in attempting to answer the question which every practising headteacher has asked at some time or another in these kinds of situations: 'How do I handle this one?' In seeking to answer this question, the following elements are covered:

- key messages from the analysis of dilemmas;
- a model process for dealing with a dilemma (the dilemma toolkit) comprising:

  a. underlying themes which underpin every situation of 'dilemma';

  b. a sequential process to assist decision making and action taking.

- a worked example of the toolkit in action.

Key messages from the analysis of dilemmas

Does any of what has been discussed so far in this short summary text help a headteacher to confront his or her dilemmas? There is a substantial literature in the field of dilemmas, as we have seen. Much of this has been concerned to describe their existence and the problems they can create (e.g. underprepared and overstressed school headteachers!).

Comparatively few accounts go on to recommend how headteachers should develop their skills in this area. Dempster and Mahony (1998) tried to tap into headteachers' practical knowledge, with limited success. Many of the studies quoted showed interest in how headteachers interpreted the dilemma situations, describing and analysing their ethical and/ or political reasoning. The linked series of works of Shapiro and Stefkovich (2001), Furman (2004) and Stevkovich and O'Brien (2004), building on earlier work by Strike *et al.* (1988) and Starrat (1994) develop useful frames from which to explore what is at stake in the different dilemma situations they describe. However, as we have already seen, their ethical framing, valuable as it is, is at best a support for useful dialogue among practising professionals, helping them to analyse the problems and possible solutions and to reflect and to learn with and from each other. The best place from which to obtain an overview of the field is in the extensive collections of essays and articles on this theme put together by Paul Begley and others (Jacobson *et al.*, 1996; Begley, 1999a, 2004a; Begley and Leonard, 1999; Begley and Johansson, 2003). Here we see an international community of academics, many with a responsibility for running programmes aimed at preparing headteachers for their duties, talking to each other about what they have found in their research and in their teaching about the key issues that need to be considered. These authorities provide a hugely rich description and analysis of the contemporary school in the plural developed democracies of the English-speaking world and Scandinavia. The complex picture painted by them does justice to the political and ethical complexity of learning how to live with other people in community (for all of us) and of learning in relation to schooling in particular (for those who work in schools). While these studies map the territory, there is no easy formula which can be applied to a dilemma situation.

It is in specific situations that the knowledgeable and experienced professional brings to bear all the perspectives involved. In the world of professional practice, as opposed to the university, judgement is not just an observation but an action. There seems to be more practical action-focused advice in the field of medical or business ethics than in educational leadership preparation. General studies of the development and practice of professional judgement such as those of Callahan (1988), Rest and Narváez (1994) and Lawrence (1999) have, for example, a clearer and more focused approach in the medical and paramedical field. The collection edited by Fish and Coles (1998) describes itself as being based on 'intensive practitioner research', the aim of which is to uncover in detail the 'artistry' of the skilled professional in order to enhance understanding of practice and judgement. The same type of texts and collections are readily found in the world of business.[1] This wider literature often supports 'case-based' approaches to professional understanding. In school leadership, 'cases' are not technical problems with an agreed 'bottom line'. They are situated in complex, many layered human situations, set in specific interactive contexts, often complicated by the confused plurality of contemporary living and the multiple goals of education.

In my time as a 'headteacher developer', running programmes at the University of Edinburgh and in partnership with colleagues in the profession, I made various attempts at creating the kind of practical model which would assist headteachers in dealing with dilemmas. There was partial success, as the following examples illustrate:

1. In workshop settings, whether within the formal training setting of SQH, or in other training and development events involving experienced headteachers, participants always appreciated the creation of a 'communicative space', where they could discuss together and learn from each other, in relation to cases from their experience, or stimuli provided in the form of 'vignettes'.

2. The SQH programme contains, as an important part of the learning model, one-to-one coaching and support provided by the headteacher 'supporter' and by a university tutor. This model creates a space for discussion of difficult decisions with an experienced colleague. Reflection on 'critical incidents' (Tripp, 1993), whether alone or with others, also offered opportunities for complex, layered discussion and learning.

However, these opportunities were partial, often reactive settings, which depended for their success on the sharing of tacit knowledge in discussion, without a strong structural frame to make sense of the situation and articulate its wider resonances. The participants, in other words, like many of those involved in the research studies quoted above, used the professional language of their context to analyse, interpret and make decisions.

Although the model devised and successfully used by Shapiro and Stefkovich (2001) raises discussion to another level, it also seems to leave things too much to chance. A well worked through common basis seems to be essential if we are to guard against a 'pick'n'mix' approach to ethical discussion, in which the larder of moral philosophy and ethical discussion is raided to provided 'after the event' rationalisations of personal preferences or actions, sticking a veneer of ethical discussion over what are essentially preferential or political motivations, or succumbing to the dangers of 'principilism' (Clauser and Gert, 1990). The communicative space which we need is neither a blank canvas, with no reference to previous thinking, nor randomly constructed, with reference only to the perspectives a particular group of people happen to bring to the table.

The first four chapters of this book provided an overview of issues in learning and identity, the politics of schooling and the ethics of human decisions and actions. These viewpoints overlap. Each has suggested that in a complex plural society, individuals bring different cognitive interpretations, often supported by strong emotional attachments, to any situation. Part of the solution must therefore involve a space where individuals can develop understanding together, as a collective, not an individual enterprise. Headteachers must be involved in some way in the creation and maintenance of such a space. It is a space in which people do not just relate to an abstract set of ideas or principles, worthy as these may be, but relate to each other as individuals in a community, creating a community of trust and shared intention. Trust is a necessary lubricant, ensuring that the differences of view and opinion which are an inescapable part of relationships do not become major sources of conflict.

Any 'toolkit' which would support the headteacher in creating such a space could not be based on an individualising model of professional practice (for example helping the headteacher clarify his or her views as an isolated individual, reflecting in the study at night, or in peer discussions with colleagues), but ensure that the headteachers' understandings engage with those held in the community. Nor could it support random or contingent sense-making: that is, your decisions and priorities would be decided by who you happen to know, or what you happen to have read, or what 'principles' for decision making you had found most congenial, or who in your community argued the most convincing case, or had the most political power. There would have to be a degree of objectivity about the process, so that any headteacher, in whatever situation, would have access to the same conceptual resources in helping them to respond well to the dilemmas they faced. Relativism is not an option (Nussbaum, 1993).

The 'toolkit' which follows results from professional use and discussion and aims to meet the following professional criteria:

- comprehensive and generalisable (useable in all situations);
- short and easy to follow (my ambition was to summarise the process on to one page – however, its execution might well be extensive in any given situation);
- intellectually robust in its analysis (it fairly represents the complex reality of the dilemma situation);
- educational (it fulfils an educational role in helping all those involved to learn more about living and making decisions about how to live).

The 'notes of explanation' which support the use of the toolkit are, in essence, the text of this book so far. Thus an approach into the dilemma which only acknowledged 'ethical' frames of reference would not sufficiently meet the practical requirements which often face headteachers. If indeed, as I have argued, judgement requires both ethics and politics, informed by an understanding of how human beings perceive and learn individually and socially, these three frames of reference need always to be near the surface. The toolkit therefore not only provides a structure within which a learning discussion can take place, but also points to earlier sources of understanding and practice on which that structure can or should be built.

The toolkit in its present form is a work in progress. There are inherent tensions in the exercise which ensure it can never be completed: comprehensive but able to be specific; intellectually robust but brief; practical but analytical. By publishing to the community of professional educators, I invite dialogue and practical improvement. At the very least, as a practical aid, it provides a set of signposts for action, pointing out the route to be followed, providing symbols and categories to help interpretation. In the first part, some underlying themes which run through every dilemma-type situation are highlighted. The headteacher's actions in relation to these themes create a favourable environment for dealing with a dilemma. The second part consists of an action framework, similar to many rational decision-making frameworks, in which the process of responding to a dilemma is outlined in sequential form in sections covering definition, exploration of options, actions and evaluation. In the worked example which follows, the quick decision making of an experienced headteacher is described. The process of her reaching her judgement is analysed in the terms of the toolkit, not in the detailed language of perception, politics or ethics. Readers may wish to undertake a more detailed analysis, using these three lenses, as a reflective response to the example.

The dilemma toolkit 1: underlying themes

Some themes have emerged from the overview of dilemmas presented through the first four chapters. These are woven into the fabric of any dilemma and headteachers require to engage with these themes as a key part of their professional practice.

1. Any dilemma involves both individuals and the school community as a whole.

2. Among the factors at stake for the school community as a whole are:
   - increase or erosion of trust in the headteacher's judgement;
   - public perceptions of the values espoused by the school;
   - educational lessons about how people should communicate to resolve their necessary differences while they live together in community;
   - educational lessons about how people in fact communicate to resolve their necessary differences while they live together in community.

3. Different individuals involved bring different frames of reference to the situation:
   - different interpretations, both cognitive and (sometimes intensely) emotional;
   - differing levels of trust of others;
   - different values;
   - different desired outcomes;
   - different view of responsibility, both in causing and resolving the situation.

4. The headteacher needs to be aware of and pay attention to his or her own role in the dilemma. Important activities for the headteacher include:

- understanding and nurturing their own character (as expressed in the kinds of virtuous personal and professional dispositions which assist in making defensible practical judgements which are trusted by others);
- maintaining sources of support and triangulation, cognitively and emotionally, to check out their understanding of what is happening from all angles; it is particularly important to check your understanding where you are dealing with a new situation or one in which there are high stakes (for the individuals, for yourself, or for the community of the school).
- building their own knowledge and understanding of the ethical and political influences affecting individuals, using the kinds of resources referenced in this text, while also building the technical skills to solve problems before they become dilemmas;
- maintaining empathy with all involved, whatever the rights and wrongs of the situation;
- being aware of the expectations others have of their behaviour and the judgements they make about their trustworthiness as the situation progresses.

5. Ultimately, the headteacher has a responsibility, within limits (Martin, 2002), for ensuring the consistent application of a well founded process, which commands the trust of the community, for the resolution of those difficult situations which have been characterised as dilemmas.

The dilemma toolkit 2: decision making and action taking

Table 5.1 **The dilemma toolkit 2**

1. Understand what you're dealing with	
Area for clarification	Questions for consideration
Construction	Is this a dilemma at all or is it a technical problem? Can technical skill reduce the space between the 'horns' of the dilemma? Is there a bureaucratic work directive which I should follow? For whom is this a dilemma – internal to you or external in the community?
Values	What values do the actors hold? (include your own) How do these fit / conflict with the agreed / public values of the school?
Power	What power do you hold? What interests, roles and power do the other actors hold?

Table 5.1 **The dilemma toolkit 2** *(continued)*

Responsibility	Who carries what responsibilities in this situation? You (with reference to different roles you (may) play)? The other parties involved? Who do they think is responsible? Other relevant players (school governors, local education authority…)?
Outcomes – learning, interests, values	What are the best outcomes of this situation in each of these three areas for each of the individuals? For the school community as a whole?

2. Explore your options	
Possible options	*These apply either to the headteacher's dilemmas or to those involving other parties and should be considered sequentially as required.*
Who is involved?	What is the role of the different individuals involved in arriving at a best decision'? Should I play a neutral role? Should I call on any others who might assist e.g. playing a 'neutral' trustworthy role if I am too easily seen as partial? What responsibilities are parties involved willing to accept?
Principled stance	Are there any absolutes for me in this situation – principles or issues which are so important that I (or others) cannot or will not concede? Is holding to these principles more important than looking for agreed solutions? Can these values be upheld, yet an agreed solution be reached?
Agreement on core values	Can all parties agree to accept certain core values (e.g. that all the children involved should continue to have access to a full education in their community?). Does this give a starting-point?
Conflict resolution	Voluntary engagement in conflict resolution (e.g. mediation, restorative practice).
Compromise through negotiation	Try win–win negotiating options, through principled negotiation which accepts the integrity of the other's position as a starting-point. An acceptable solution is one in which both parties are happy with the outcome.
Imposed solution	If unsuccessful, revert to win–lose solution, imposing the 'best solution'
Take no action	Allow the logic of the situation / nature / the people involved to sort it out their own way without further intervention.
Evaluation of options	*For all options that are possible and desirable*
Ethical evaluation	Is the option consistent with what you would expect of a wise and virtuous practitioner? Is the option consistent with the underlying values of schooling in a democratic society? If your preferred option of necessity infringes any underlying values (values in competition), have you reasoned it out and discussed with another wise and virtuous practitioner?

Consequences for individuals	For each action, consider the consequences in terms of their impact on the individuals involved, including yourself. What is the likelihood of each possible consequence?
Consequences for the school community	What messages does each option give about your values and/or the values of the school? Might any further problems arise? What implications does this case have for any future similar cases? Has trust been increased or decreased? Has the 'communicative space' been protected or closed off?
Consequences for the child	Are there any special interests of the child in this particular situation which are more important than anything else?

3. Take action

Why?	The prior evaluation should provide you with a robust answer to this question based on: • the fundamental values of democratic schooling; • the resolution of competing values required (if appropriate); • the consequences of the action for all involved (in particular but not exclusively for the child at the centre); • the consequences for the community of the school; and • the status of this action as the best possible in the circumstances (after consideration of all other options).
Who?	Who needs to be involved and what preparation is required to ensure that they have the skills and knowledge to fulfil their role?
Does what?	A listing of the actions to be taken and their sequence.
How?	The manner of the actions and communication involved: attention to be given to relational aspects and feelings of those involved as well as the cognitive framing and description of the process.
Communication	Who needs to know what (values / process / outcomes) so that the values and integrity of the community (and the headteacher as its agent) are reinforced and supported, or challenged and improved through learning?

4. Evaluate after the event

Understanding	Was the analysis sound? Can you account for any gaps?
Responsibility	Did those involved have the appropriate share in the responsibility? What did they learn in and from the situation?
Consequences	What was the impact on the individuals? (values, interests, perceptions of self and community) What was the impact on the community? (values, processes, common understandings and learning) What was the impact on you? (character, leadership power (given by others) sense of self-efficacy)
Building an ethical community	Were consistent trustworthy patterns of principled behaviour further reinforced? Was the communicative space protected and enhanced?
Communication	What was the 'public' perception of these matters? Could it have been improved? What was the impact of public perception on the overall outcome for the school community?

In the worked example which follows, we see an experienced headteacher making decisions about an everyday school situation, without reference to a 'toolkit', but understanding the complexity of the situation and assessing risks and consequences in the short timeframe available.

Vignette 6

A teacher raises her voice to two large adolescent pupils in the corridor. She feels justified in this because the pupils have been running towards a junction and she has seen accidents caused in the past when pupils running in this way have collided with smaller pupils walking round the corner. From the teacher's viewpoint, she has taken responsibility, despite the fact that these boys are quite tall. If she had to engage every pupil in discussion about the issues rather than making an authoritative declaration she would never manage to do anything. The pupils, however, are incensed. They feel that they should be treated as young adults and that the teacher's shouting at them shows a lack of respect. They blame the teacher for picking on them, an understanding which fits well into the way they feel teachers in the school generally view them. Before they would be willing to listen to and understand the teacher's motivation, they want to be given the respect which they feel is their right and their due. They argue back to the teacher, making clear their lack of respect for someone who does not respect them (as they see it). The teacher then imposes a formal detention. The boys refuse to do the detention, making clear their contempt for the teacher and any authority she is trying to impose. The teacher then brings the case to the Headteacher. The headteacher feels that if she supports the teacher the boys will be confirmed in their view of school as a hostile place, which does not value them. On the other hand, not to support the teacher would contribute to the school becoming a more disorderly place and give the wrong messages to staff.

The headteacher knows that if she does not fully support the teacher, the teacher may not take responsibility in a similar situation again. On the other hand, supporting the teacher, she believes, will contribute to the alienation of the pupils involved…and alienated pupils are less likely to engage with the school's commitment to their learning.

Worked example

Understanding the problem

In responding to this situation, the headteacher took some time to analyse what had happened and what was at stake. The initial incident was a straightforward exercise of power vested in teachers to ensure safety in school. However, it had been overlaid with an interpersonal conflict, in which both parties had taken exception to what they perceived as disrespect on the part of the other party. The emotional responses on both sides at the time of the incident had intensified these feelings and increased tension, and made this into a 'high stakes' incident for both parties. The teacher gave a straightforward account of the events, blamed both boys equally and wanted to be 'backed up'. If she were not, it might erode her confidence to deal with similar incidents (for example she might 'retreat' into her classroom and hide from responsibility for safe movement in corridors). Moreover if she retailed the story in a certain way in the staffroom, the headteacher might find many teachers questioning their position on these matters ('We're supposed to take action, but when we do we get no back up . . .'). On the other hand, the headteacher suspects that both boys were not equally involved and without investigating yet, believes it likely that although both were running, the aggressive reaction to the situation will have come from one of the boys in particular. If the teacher might have that fact wrong, has she got other facts wrong? If on the other hand the headteacher conducts an investigation into the incident to ascertain the 'facts' independently (seeking witnesses, etc.), she is aware that this will be seen by the teacher as very stressful ('You think you're doing the right thing, then it turns out you're on the receiving end of an inquisition . . . '). The headteacher is aware that this teacher is in a very brittle position emotionally with her life at present. She has gone through a difficult marital breakup within the past two years, which has had a big impact on her general outlook on life, while the long-term support and care of her mother, who lives alone, some distance away and is steadily declining in capacity also causes a strain. Recently another member of staff in a neighbouring part of the school, with apparently fewer personal problems deriving from a difficult family situation, was signed off on long-term sick leave with 'stress'. This has been the subject of some conversation in the staffroom, especially since there has been no replacement teacher and so all colleagues are having to do extra work to keep this teacher's classes going. If the teacher involved in this incident were to go off ill with stress, it would cause similar problems to the remaining members of the staff team.

On the other hand, the two pupils involved felt that they had been made to look small in front of peers. The teacher's tone of voice and manner had made clear that she treated them as 'silly wee boys', which they had felt was deeply hurtful. Both boys have a high status outside of school, where they are members of a highly successful local football team and are used to high levels of adult respect. In general their behaviour around the school is not bad. They have in the past got into some scrapes, and their profile is not particularly supportive of school values, but they have been 'talked round' before. One set of parents is very supportive of the school. The other parents, however, are very confrontational and often in the past have said that the school 'picks on' their son. He has been more vociferous and challenging on one or two occasions in the past. The emotional reaction of the boys acted as a 'challenge' to the teacher, who has responded by upping the stakes, as they were challenging her authority in the school. The headteacher is aware that, if she takes a straightforwardly authoritarian approach with the boys, that this may be seen as yet another instance of the school acting as an alienating external authority, a message which the boys and their parents will reinforce in the community. She will also face a confrontation with at least one of the sets of parents, who in the past have taken this kind of incident to the local authority to complain. This will create more time pressures for her as if a complaint goes through, she will have to participate in an investigation and attend resolution meetings.

The headteacher believes the other parties have transferred responsibility for the incident to her and now will interpret her judgement in the light of their own (partial) frames of reference. She separates the incident into two parts: running in the corridor (against a well rehearsed school rule); a tense exchange between two pupils and a member of staff in which they questioned her authority in an aggressive and public manner. She does not conceptualise the situation in terms of care, justice, critique or community, although if pressed could uncover these concepts. These are not terms which are familiar to the other parties involved and cannot be easily used in the forthcoming disussions with them. There is a degree of time pressure on the situation. As an experienced headteacher, she has already met this situation in several similar incidents. One aspect of the culture in the local area is that many of the parents did not do particularly well when they were at school and see schooling as a service done to them by the state, rather a service they engage with, to get the best for their children. To some extent culturally alienated from the school, and therefore seeing themselves as 'powerless', students often complain of being unfairly treated. Although this is a high stakes situation for the parties involved, the headteacher has a number of interviews to conduct in the current week, has a meeting out of school with other local headteachers on proposed local authority restructuring and has a full diary on top. She also has a major report to complete for her local authority by the end of the week. Her own domestic diary is problematic this week. Her older daughter, a student at a university some 100 miles distant, is experiencing a bit of a personal crisis and wants to come home for the rest of the week and will undoubtedly want time. Her husband is working long hours just now.

The headteacher considers what she would do in an ideal scenario, but assessing the risk if this going wrong, decides to go for a safer option, which she nonetheless believes balances out the competing interests, while protecting key school community values. Both her ideal and her actual decision processes are now summarised below.

In her *ideal* scenario, the headteacher tries to resolve the matter quickly, in a manner which shows emotional support for all parties, but allows some learning to take place on all sides and secures the important messages about safety in the corridors which the teacher had been attempting to get over. She has a separate conversation with each of the parties involved. She persuades both boys that they have committed an offence, and the more aggressive of the two that he has committed two offences. She agrees that they deserve respect and reassures them that it is because the teacher respects all pupils in the school that she takes clear responsibility to enforce rules aimed at ensuring pupil safety. She invites the boys to participate in agreeing what is an appropriate punishment or restorative action (a) for the initial offence (b) for the distress caused to the teacher by their aggressive response. She also has a private conversation with the teacher. She explains that she is very pleased that the teacher has taken responsibility for ensuring pupil safety and commends her for it. She also explains that the issue for the boys was not to do with content but with manner and that the headteacher does consider the issue of 'respect' to be an important one in the school. She is sure that the teacher in no way intended disrespect, but communication is about what the listener understands, not just what the speaker intends. She reminds the teacher that the school policy is to sandwich every negative within two positives, and that on another occasion, by assuring the pupils that she knows they are old enough to understand the reasons for safety rules before she calls them up, she will have more success. She asks the teacher if she wants to have a meeting with the boys, to 'tidy matters up'. In the meeting the boys will be invited to accept fault and to apologise for any upset caused to the teacher. The teacher will also have an opportunity to show respect to the boys as people, while also making clear her disapproval of their actions. She will also be supported by the headteacher for her action in promoting safe movement. She closes by reminding the teacher that she really values what she does around the school – it makes a difference. In this ideal scenario, the headteacher hopes that the restorative meeting and the actions around it will restore relationships, while also reinforcing the school rules about movement, supporting the teacher in enforcing these rules, and also helping all parties to learn about their responsibility for the situation which arose. She believes that if the more assertive of the two boys accepts this solution, his parents will not get involved. She believes this is also the best solution in the interests of the students involved, as they need to know that the school, as a community, needs a system of rules to codify the responsibilities which each individual owes to others. Not reinforcing the rules clearly would give the impression that if you shout loud enough, and/ or aggressively enough, you can avoid your responsibilities. This would be a bad message for the boys and a bad message for the community.

Exploring options

The headteacher is aware she has a number of other options and explores these largely in terms of their consequences for the individuals involved and for the school community, including its 'ethical' character and the 'learning' she hopes will come from the incident. She does not use an exact calculus to evaluate these options. It is a question of her experienced judgement (her 'knowledge-in-action' Schon, 1987). However, she does have a 'rule of thumb' that both scale and likelihood are important factors in assessing the risks and benefits of particular courses of action.

The 'ideal' option for this headteacher as outlined above carries some risks. Although she believes that it may offer the best learning outcomes from the situation, she is also aware that it could go badly wrong if the other parties involved do not accept responsibility for a solution. She has experience in relation to previous incidents of 'worst case' outcomes spiralling out of control from similar small beginnings. Worst outcomes might begin with the teacher, mistrustful, interpreting the actions of the headteacher as accusatory. Scared of the headteacher's potential power in the situation (for example, that an investigation might lead to the teacher being disciplined for shouting at the pupils), the teacher might retreat into defensive mode, refuse to meet the headteacher except with her union representative present and interpret the whole situation as the final straw in the collapse of good order within society in general and the school in particular. Staffroom gossip will support the teacher's view and undermine the headteacher's credibility with her staff, who then lose trust in her with consequently bad effects on the overall quality of teamwork in the school. In the various tense meetings with staff, pupils and parents over this incident, an already full diary overflows and the headteacher has to stay at work to complete the report, losing time she had wanted to have for her daughter, with associated feelings of guilt. She begins to doubt if this is a job she can do and begins to dread coming into school, as she is bothered by what she thinks staff might be saying behind her back. In an even worse case scenario, this incident and the headteacher's response might be, for the teacher involved, 'the straw that breaks the camel's back'. Under personal pressure from situations outwith work, the stress causes her to go to her doctor who immediately signs her off work. She is unable to return for some time, during which period, numerous problems arise with the classes. Frequent complaints and several desperate adverts in the national press fail to produce a teacher, but occupy significant amounts of personal and emotional energy for all involved. The subject leader, run ragged trying to teach his own classes and also to set and mark work for the class of the teacher who is off with stress, is unable to undertake his normal quality assurance activities within the team and he himself is becoming overstressed.

In this worst case scenario, the more assertive of the two boys refuses to back off despite the headteacher's personal chat. He challenges the school to take further action. The headteacher has an extended meeting with the parents, in which they accuse her of unfair behaviour. They say that the headteacher should be disciplining the member of staff for picking on their son, rather than disciplining their son. His classmate now supports his account that they were not really running anyway, just 'walking quickly'.

The headteacher reluctantly excludes the boy since both he and his parents have refused to accept the disciplinary requirements of the school (one of the legal bases of exclusion in the Scottish system). However, the parents appeal, leading to extensive legalistic meetings within the school and at authority level. During the period of appeal the boy remains in school and meetings of staff are held, looking for support from their union for a refusal to teach the boy concerned, who makes it clear by a rather arrogant and sneering manner that he has 'got one over on the school', something which seems to drive up the blood pressure of a large number of staff. The appeals committee upholds the appeal because the headteacher, in their view, did not conduct an entirely independent investigation into the initial offence. At its extreme, this worst case outcome then exposes and reinforces the divisions and tensions of the school to no one's apparent benefit.

From this risk assessment, she decides to keep a tighter control herself of her response, by using her authority, rationalising this as an ethical position as it reduces risks of worse outcomes.

Take action

The headteacher calls in the boys and gives them a chance to account for their behaviour. She clearly reinforces the teachers' actions and explains that the teacher is within her rights to discipline the boys for unacceptable behaviour. She expects them to complete their punishment and they will face further consequences if they do not. She sandwiches this message with two positive statements about their general behaviour, clearly separating her respect for the boys from her attitudes to this particular behaviour. She agrees with the boys that in general teachers should not shout at pupils, though they may need to if they feel they are not being heard, of if they feel pupils are not taking the matters raised seriously and want a 'shorthand' way of saying 'this matters'. She agrees to take this up with the individual staff member. She tells the teacher she has fully supported her and asks her to have a word with the boys next time she sees them to show her respect for them, 'perhaps 'a jokey word if she sees them in the corridor and they are walking?' She briefs staff on the incident and the need to 'keep calm' with pupils. She reinforces the key message about corridor safety, and how students should speak to staff, at pupil assemblies. She is prepared to listen to the parents if required, but does not allow space in her busy diary for this week. She protects her own time for her daughter and feels good about how she is doing her job.

Evaluate the outcomes

Understanding
As an experienced headteacher, she feels that she has a good grasp of the practical situation. She has not used the language of learning theory, ethics,

or of organisational behaviour or micropolitics to interpret and articulate this, and might not have as full an overview on another occasion, perhaps in less familiar territory. Nonetheless her viewpoint does cover in a rounded way the range of issues at stake in the situation and can be seen as politically astute and ethically based.

Responsibility

The headteacher believes that some of the responsibility for this incident should be shared by the participants, but considers that none of the participants has the capacity to do that independently and that the risks of inviting them to share responsibility could easily outweigh the benefits. She therefore accepts the responsibility they want to give to her.

Consequences

Good order and respectful relationships have been reinforced. There is a danger that teachers may feel that they can behave outwith school rules and still be backed up by the headteacher, but she has covered that with an individual and whole staff briefing. There is a danger that the pupils will become further alienated but she has made clear that she respects them and wants them to play their part in the community. It is this particular behaviour which was unacceptable. There is a danger that the message for the school community may be that the school is authoritarian, but she covers that by the tone and character of her message to pupils in assembly.

Building an ethical community

The school community has had some key messages about rights and obligations reinforced. Safety has been emphasised as a key concern of all in school. Staff meetings, school assemblies and the student council have the chance to review school rules.

Communication

There are risks in the public perception of these events. Students involved may, for example, negatively brief their friends and parents, and perhaps others in the community, about the unfair character of the school community and how it works to their disadvantage. The headteacher has no control over this communication, nor does she have an opportunity to refute misinformation about what happened or the intentions behind it. This is true, however, of any of the alternatives. She hopes that this incident communicates clear messages about her intentions and is consistent with other messages that she has given through how she dealt with other incidents. She hopes that these are trustworthy messages that will inspire greater trust and security in the future. However, these are hopes, rather than firm conclusions on the outcome. By the next day, this incident has faded into the background as a number of new matters have assumed priority.

The reader may now wish to examine this case study through the different lenses offered in this book:

- What did the individuals involve 'learn' (if anything) about each other and about their responsibilities?
- Who had power in this situation, what might trigger the use of power and what power was actually used?
- How might the headteacher's behaviour be described in ethical terms? Were there any issues of absolute principle involved (a) for the headteacher (b) for any of the other participants?
- What types of trust are seen in this case? Was trust increased, reduced, or unaffected?

Note

1 As a starting-point for access to works in this field within the massive literature supporting MBAs, see for example Kakabadse and Kakabadse (1999) or Nielsen (1996). For 'principled negotiation' start with Fisher (1989). Johnson (2001) contains a cornucopia of different possible approaches to ethical decision making. Within a broadly spiritual framework ('good and evil') he pulls together a range of case studies and different approaches – there is something of value for most 'leaders' in this rich set of resources.

Chapter 6

POLICIES AND PRACTICES:
WIDER IMPLICATIONS

Chapter 1 showed how the experience of dealing with dilemmas is a characteristic feature of contemporary school leadership. Chapters 2 to 4 looked at these dilemmas through three different lenses. In Chapter 5 these insights were brought together in recommendations about building trust within school communities, a trust which helps people come together to look for solutions. Even where there is a rich fabric of trust, dilemmas may arise. A sequential process for responding to a dilemma was therefore outlined, and a worked example was provided. In this final chapter, a number of policy and practice implications are explored, beginning with the specific case of the headteacher, leading to more general issues of public service and citizenship in a plural democracy.

The role and responsibilities of the headteacher

Implications for the role and responsibilities of the headteacher are described and analysed under four headings:

- know yourself and know others;
- definition;
- accountability;
- training and support.

Know yourself and know others

This section is addressed to headteachers and aspirant headteachers alike. Earlier discussion has established that decision making must have ethical and political dimensions, but that this is more than simple political manoeuvring or picking ethical principles to fit what you had already decided. It concerns the person and what that individual is seen to value. Character matters: integrity, trustworthy behaviour, wisdom, honesty, good intentions, willingness to learn. As someone skilled in developing good relationships, in an atmosphere which builds trust in the intentions and competence of others, you can help people to overcome differences in their values and interests. You are less likely to be surprised by forces outwith your control if you know where power lies and how it is being used, both by those within the school community and those beyond it. You also need to understand both your emotional responses, particularly where these may be intense, and your cognitive biases – your predisposition to frame events in particular ways. Whatever you may feel, you are not alone. There are people able to help you check your own perception of the situation. If there is no knowledgeable person to hand, you can still call on a substantial international literature, referenced in this short text, which can provide insight and understanding, connecting you to a much wider group of people, in your own society and in others, who have thought through the same problems and issues.

It is necessary but not sufficient for you to know about yourself. You need to know and understand the cognitive biases and the emotions of others. Are there gaps in their understanding? Who do they trust and who do they mistrust? For headteachers, professionals in 'learning', considering how emotion and cognitive bias enables or obstructs learning should be second nature. These implications for the headteacher or aspirant headteacher require a considerable degree of self-awareness and awareness of the role and responsibilities of the job – but is there agreement on what these are?

Defining the work of the headteacher

Beyond the bland generalisations of specific job descriptions, professional understanding of the work of headteachers is summarised in a variety of national Standards (Standards for School Leaders, 2007). The Standard for Headship in Scotland (SEED, 2005) provides a rich definition of headship as a dynamic situation-specific professional activity, involving a range of skills, managerial competences and educational values. Contemporary aspirational accounts of school leadership in the international literature are often inspiring. A particular favourite of mine is the account in Joseph Murphy (2002), where the school principal is seen as an 'educator', a 'community builder' and a 'moral steward'. Are these aspirations achievable? The surveys quoted in Chapter 1 suggest a considerable discontinuity between employer expectations and what headteachers feel is possible. The more limited but intensive study of McEwen *et al.* (2000) confirms that headteachers are never far from a descent into a 'milieu of immediacy dominated by low and middle order priorities' (p. 239). Official job descriptions can be very open ended. The overworked, sometimes role-confused headteachers that took part in these studies live in a Mintzbergian (Mintzberg, 1975) world of constant interruption and microdecision, with no time for reflection and coherent strategic thinking. Gronn's (Gronn, 2003) notion of 'greedy work' captures well this 'limitless' character of role expectations. Expectations of schools have outstripped all reality. Professional staff strive to bridge this gap between expectations and reality at personal cost. The social context of these stresses is an important factor. In well supported social situations, with shared understanding and team collegiallity with co-workers, stress can help ensure there is no complacency and fuel a desire for constant improvement within the boundaries of what is achievable. But where unsupported, the job can feel impossible. As one headteacher feeling herself under pressure put it to me, 'We don't expect surgeons to cure every patient . . . people die despite medical intervention, yet it feels like every child who fails at school is failed by me . . .'.

A strong recent theme in the Scottish policy community picking up the indeterminate character of the job has been to emphasise the importance of 'collegial leadership' within a school community (COSLA, n d). Leadership goes beyond management. It makes sense out of complexity, empowers and involves others, applies broader understanding to a local situation and agrees actions with those involved – leadership but with the agreement of those being led: a paradox of democratic leadership (Riley, 2002). Headteachers cannot be just 'branch managers' of a local education service, performing to a set of bureaucratic instructions, but have to embrace the wider social confusions of the postmodern age in leading an educational community. A Headteacher who sits tight on what the law, or their particular job contract, requires and defines the roles of others according to structure, will rapidly be swamped by the indeterminacy which they hope to avoid.

The theme of 'redefining' leadership relates closely to current thinking on redefining the teaching profession as a whole, and, more widely yet, the redefinition of schooling itself. In Scotland recently, the national curriculum review group has reclaimed schooling from a narrow focus on academic attainment, defining the key outcomes of schooling in terms of the four capacities of the citizen of the future: 'successful learner, confident individual, effective contributor and responsible citizen' (SEED, n d). Yet this welcome rebalancing retains too narrow a focus on the individual. Where are the needs of the often 'taken for granted' community. Individuals cannot develop in an impoverished community. School teaching and school leadership necessarily have a strong role in building community, whether they choose to structure and articulate this role, or allow it to happen by default. The relationships which characterise the interpersonal exchanges of the school community contribute powerfully to the socialisation of young people into a particular way of being with other people. The school may be the place where the child's sense of community, however inadequate, is best found. The sense of community in a school cannot be taken for granted. School communities can be fragmented by unequal distributions of power and influence, or different competing values. The appearance of stability in the school as an institution, housed in a solid building, can hide powerful destructive forces, pulling at the sense of community in people's minds. The tensions and lack of community characteristic of some schools, and the consequent failure to engage its learners, have led to a political frustration that schools appear unable to deliver for *all* our young people.

Should headteachers accept all the responsibilities which these broad and inspiring definitions of school leadership demand? It is often tempting, in more uncertain situations, for an individual to whom a difficult problem has been referred to assume responsibility but this sometimes needs to be resisted, else they may fall prey to the 'responsibility virus' (Martin, 2002). Martin argues effectively that taking responsibility away from others is often an ineffective way of making important decisions. 'The Responsibility Virus produces hopeless failures resulting from extreme mismatches of capabilities and responsibilities, which leads to cover up rather than learning' (pp. 268–9).

It can be too tempting for a headteacher, who occupies an office to which difficult referrals often take place and from which an overview of the complex competing forces of contemporary community can be observed, to assume the responsibility for 'sorting' problems. Before taking responsibility, headteachers need to define the responsibilities of other people involved. If the headteacher exercises a power of decision, are they removing it from others? Should others see more sides of a problem? Should others accept complexity in the situation? Should others be willing to contribute to the solution? This is true in the individual case (a dilemma) and in the general case (widely varying civic opinions about how the community should socialise its children). But wanting responsibility is, in my experience, an endemic condition of the headteacher – it is why they applied for the job in the first place. One of the reasons headteachers may want to assume more responsibility is because they are held accountable. Being held accountable for doing your best to implement someone else's poor policy requirements (*they* are responsible, but *you* are accountable) is not a pleasant experience. To paraphrase Mr Micawber, 'responsibility 60%, accountability 40%, result "happiness"; responsibility 40%, accountability 60%, result "misery".' What then of accountability?

The accountability of headteachers

Headteachers have multiple accountabilities. They are *professionally* accountable to the 'clients' of their service – the children, parents and staff who share in the school community which they lead. In Scotland, the Standards in Scotland's Schools etc. Act (SEED, 2000a) recognised a more complex set of relationships and accountabilities to parents and pupils than is yet represented in 'official statistics'. However, headteachers are also *politically and contractually* accountable as employees, through a system of school governance, to governors and/or to public officers of political authorities. The tangled web of these interacting forces makes different demands. Sometimes these different lines of accountability cause dilemmas: which client should the headteacher serve, victim or accused (Vignette 3), child or employer (Vignette 4)? Is there a limit to the accountability the headteacher can or should accept? In the words of the recent reframing of accountability in Scotland, are the accountabilities sufficiently 'intelligent' (SEED, 2004)?

Certainly, in common with other developed school systems, the official, external accountability of the Scottish system through national measures of academic attainment has in the past been too simple and also simply inaccurate. Moreover key stakeholders, with different values and concepts of schooling, have many different goals for schooling beyond academic attainment, and some of these goals may pull against each other (Lunt and Norwich, 1999).

Karen Riley (1998) describes a process by which children in one North London school defined the accountabilities of their ideal headteacher:

> If you are going to apply for this job, you will need to be able to communicate with children, be respectful of them and understand their point of view. You will need to be well qualified and experienced. You will need to be energetic, outgoing, confident, mix with people easily and understand their feelings. You will need to understand people's beliefs and be a calming influence on the school. (p. 122)

Most headteachers I know would happily settle for this naïve but clear statement of the kind of person who should be a headteacher! It has been argued above that primary, special and pre-5 schools, even those in very culturally diverse communities, can achieve such clarity more easily because of the priority given to an ethic of care – this comes through this clear statement of what matters in a school leader. Insulated from some of the broader social tensions which become increasingly hard to disguise as children near the threshold of the 'adult world' beyond schooling, a cocoon of care can be created. Even in the most plural of situations there can be consensual clarity of both goal and accountability around the happiness of the children, their health and wellbeing.

Earlier discussion established the role of 'choice' of school, or the perception of choice, in reducing the degree of variance of opinion *within* particular school communities. Choice in educational enrolment can, with variations in different state systems, be expressed through faith schools (and the perceived common values they support), independent schools (with an individual ethos and heritage), parental choice (the market model of schooling), or through parent-founded, government funded schools (as in several Scandinavian systems). In school systems where there are different types of school and where a large number of parents, particularly politically influential parents, can choose a particular school or their child, different social goals for schooling are represented by different types of school, rather than tensions within the same school (for futher discussion see Lawton, 2006). In school communities with little consensus on, for example, the role of the school, beyond technical aspects of classroom learning, or where there are few shared concepts about the wider social role of the school, an aspiration to 'build community' will be much harder to achieve. If, as Bryk and

Schneider maintain (2002), children thrive in school communities with the kinds of rich social capital that comes from shared values and strong relational trust, some headteachers have a much more difficult starting-point. The social task of headteachers in highly inclusive schools situated within highly differentiated societies will be significantly more challenging than for headteachers in schools with a self-selected intake reflecting more uniform social or educational values. If these responsibilities and goals are different, should the accountabilities also be different? If the development of social trust supported by democratic forms of decision making and engagement is a key element in successful schooling, should this not be a feature of the accountability? This is a more complex accountability – 'intelligent accountability' indeed.

Training and supporting headteachers

The major insights into the role of the headteacher which are summarised in this study of dilemmas also have implications for how headteachers are trained, developed and supported. Three elements are now considered:

- conceptual resources;
- university education faculties;
- types of training and support.

Conceptualising and understanding

Schools are called on to play a role in the socialisation of young people, and to some degree staff and parents, into democratic living in a world of plurality and complexity. Considering earlier discussion, a minimum curriculum for the aspirant headteacher should therefore involve:

- psychology and learning – constructivist learning theory combined with an understanding of the social character of cognition, the role of intention and emotion;
- politics and power – the accountability of schools as public institutions in a plural society; democratic principles and the role of schooling in democratic formation;
- ethics and moral formation – practice in ethical decision making, ideally based on an ethical code for the profession; the cultivation of habits of integrity; the moral formation of young people in the school community.

The first of these requirements is perhaps the easiest to satisfy. All teachers' professional training involves the development of a disciplined understanding of human cognition and the roles of language, emotion and understanding of intention in structuring cognition in certain ways. The social character of knowledge, developed through the reliable understandings of academic traditions (Moore and Young, 2001), and the necessarily social character of much cognition, rooted as it is in relationships and cultural practices, are perhaps less well covered. It could be argued that teachers' understanding of learning is not sufficiently applied to adult learning (including their own), being more focused on children's learning.

However, there is probably more of a foundation in this area than in the other two areas. The political area, for example, is dealt with quite differently within different national and school communities. Democratic formation and socialisation is at the heart of schooling, but deeply contested. Political problems are mirrored and multiplied in the application of ethical principles to current school practice. Currently the Scottish teaching profession generally, and headteachers in particular, lack a consistent and commonly understood ethical framework to assist with evaluating the complex situations encountered in schools. This lack of a shared set of concepts and language with which to frame and understand these issues is a massive problem. It is a moral vacuum at the heart of the profession. Ethical considerations are part of what it is to be a teacher (Carr, 2000). Campbell (2000, 2003) has argued successfully that while a formal ethical code is insufficient on its own to develop ethical awareness or improve ethical practice, the process of its development is an essential step on that road. A requirement to articulate and discuss ethical norms brings potentially different values to the surface; it requires teachers and headteachers to confront ethical complexity; if it leads to 'agreed standards' rooted in teaching practice and the daily dilemmas of schooling, not written by a detached individual in an 'ivory tower', such a code can 'instill moral clarity and courage in the individual teacher grappling with dilemmas and uncertainties' (Campbell, 2003, p. 122). Although an ethical code, and the internalised understandings which derive from it, might be of great importance to any individual grappling with ethical and social complexity, it would also play an important balancing role for the profession as a whole. Such a code would establish clearly, as this book has argued, that while political insights into, and responses to, the dilemmas of schooling are necessary, they are insufficient: politics must be informed by ethics if it is not to become an arbitrary contest of power. The Scottish profession lacks a fully developed ethical code for teachers and headteachers. It is an urgent requirement. Universities have an important role in working with the profession to develop such understanding.

The teaching profession and the university

Establishing an agreed 'knowledge base' for the profession of 'headteacher' is a complex and demanding challenge. It is a civic function of universities to work with professions to provide professional training and to extend our understanding of the practice of the professions, as well as our knowledge of what works in practice. The teaching profession (in particular the secondary school profession) presents particular problems. Most teachers are schooled within different academic traditions. Professions such as medicine or architecture share the same broad social concerns as teachers, but there is a common core of scholarly knowledge, and a common research method, within professional training. The academic traditions which make the greatest contributions to our understanding of the interactive social character of schooling (psychology, sociology, politics and ethics) are strange to many teachers, who have been trained within other disciplines. Without the structure of a particular academic tradition such as the scientific tradition in medicine, concepts in teaching are often used loosely, while methods can lack validity or reliability. Applied versions of psychology, evident in the development of theories about learning, do feature in the professional vocabulary and practices of teachers. In addition, there is a widespread concern with effective practice in teaching and learning. However, there is only a limited commitment to evidence-based practice and experimental method even in these areas.

There is even less potential for agreement in relation to contested areas involving politics, social enquiry or values. In the more nebulous aspects of schooling so much bound up with the role of the headteacher, such as its role in democratic formation, or how a school community responds to the moral and social complexity of its community, there is even less professional clarity. The urgency and social complexity of the teacher's and headteacher's day, and the necessity of developing a shared 'common-sense' vocabulary that children, parents and teachers can use, militate further against specialist enquiry. This issue in the development of our knowledge about the profession of teaching needs to be recognised and addressed by the profession and universities together. One part of the basis for such common engagement is outlined in the seminal works of Kolb (1984), Schon (1987) and Eraut (1994), locating the professionalism of the headteacher or teacher in a broader model of professionalism more generally, but there is much work to be done. In current interactions between university and the teaching profession in Scotland there are pockets of excellence and major gaps.

The structures supporting such developing interaction between the profession and the universities are patchy. The Research Assessment Exercise, by which the quality of research work in British universities is assessed and rewarded, appears to value academic rather than professionally focused research activity (RAE, n d) and while recent renewed emphasis and reward for 'knowledge transfer' has established a higher priority for research work with a practical focus, this is a one way street, in which the channels for the profession (as opposed to the university) to develop the new knowledge and understandings arising from daily practice are less clear. The free interaction between leading professionals and the world of research and training found, for example, in medicine or architecture is not found (yet) in teaching.

Recent work in Western Australia, which involves skilled practising school principals in developing criteria to assess how well trainee headteachers responded to difficult situations in practice, is one example of how that interaction might be better developed (Western Australia Dept of Education and Training, 2004). Another can be found in the research programmes of the National College of School Leadership in England (NCSL, n d) wich have given structured voice to professional practice, albeit outwith the independent intellectual disciplinary environment of the university. The insights gained from this study of dilemmas suggest both a degree of urgency and some further relevant first steps in that direction.

Training and supporting professional practice

Exposed to scrutiny, we now see dilemmas as a necessary consequence of plurality – plurality of interests, plurality of values and purposes, plurality of worldviews. While a strong democratic framing provides a process for deliberation and engagement, it does not point in a particular direction. In one version of this, everyone's values are important and worthy of respect, so the role of the school is not to 'impose' a particular set of values, but to allow each individual to clarify his or her own values. The 'values clarification' debates which raged across American education in the 1980s and 1990s demonstrate a strong reaction to that approach from social conservatives who argued that values are social, not individual in character (see for example Kilpatrick, 1993). 'Blindfolded in a minefield' (Dempster and Berry, 2003), the school principal needs a map of this territory.

Recent training methods applied to the development of aspirant headteachers in Scotland have combined work-based learning in managing school improvement with critical reflection (Reeves *et al.*, 2002). The analysis of dilemmas accepts that the headteacher is called on do more than 'manage', but to react to immediate complex incidents which challenge decision making, and to do so in a way which makes consistent sense of a confusing and paradoxical world. Following Kolb (1984), Schon (1987), Hallinger and Bridges (1994) and Eraut (1994), training in dealing with dilemmas would address the development of the 'knowledge-in-action' of the skilled professional, the 'beneath the surface' instant judgement by which the essential issues involved in a particular problematic situation are quickly identified and various possible actions and their potential consequences assessed. This is not just about learning techniques. Fish and Coles talk eloquently of 'professional artistry' – creative engagement with the issues is required. Moreover it has been argued from each of the key perspectives explored in Chapters 2, 3 and 4, that trust in the headteacher as a person is a vital element.

There is evidence of a variety of practice in complex decision making already in place in different school leadership training contexts (see for example Dempster *et al.*, 2002; Cardno, 1997; Strike *et al.*, 1988; Shapiro and Stefkovich, 2002). Most of the focus on dilemmas is 'ethical' in character, although most also acknowledge, as this text has emphasised, a political context and a learning dimension in any dilemma. There is also good evidence that peer discussion of 'vignettes' develops ethical thinking in professional development (Lind, 2006; Rest, 1986).[1] While no amount of ethical sensitivity can provide an absolute calculus for any individual decision, individuals who have considered the ethical as well as the political dimensions of the dilemma they face are more likely to reach a decision which they feel happy with. But if ethical analysis is to do more than provide an elaborate rationale for 'personal preference', then the profession as a whole requires to participate in ongoing ethical discussion. A professional code of ethics for the teaching profession in general and headteachers in particular is long overdue.

It is often in the nature of a school-based dilemma that all involved must participate in the analysis and the solution, if they are to learn about themselves and about the others involved. In order to have the confidence to take part, they must trust the impartiality of the public institution of the school and the professionalism of the headteacher. The democratic purposes of schools thus demand dialogue beyond the professional group (see Mulford, 2004). While in rich plural democracies this may appear as just one viewpoint among many, in the sharper political context of a post-conflict society such as Kosovo (Goddard, 2004) or a fledgling democracy such as Azerbaijan (Riley, 2002), its urgency and high priority is much more clear. It cannot be enough that the headteacher alone understands and works at these challenges. In democratic schooling, wider discussion and collegial leadership is required. The consideration of dilemmas in schooling becomes, in this way, a foundational characteristic of genuinely democratic school communities. It becomes a primary responsibility of the headteacher and one for which they need to be properly prepared and in which they need to be fully supported.

Public service and civic society

There is considerable current frustration across the UK with the inability of governments to deliver on the improvement of key public services – in particular conventional political / bureaucratic methods such as target setting and increased expenditure on new initiatives have had a limited impact, leaving a gap between expectations and what is delivered. Linear simplistic descriptions of these problems ignore their complexity and contribute to this gap. The analysis of the dilemma situations reflects the real social complexity behind the 'figures'.

Schools, whether independently or publicly funded, provide a public service. They contribute to the social capital of the community and develop its citizens' understandings of how their community works and what their responsibilities are. Socially inclusive schools go further. They provide a public space within which the community has to come to terms with tensions and differences which can be masked by separation. It is in the dilemmas found on a daily basis in these schools that the most challenging problems of contemporary social living are worked out on a daily basis. Such complex value-laden interactions are not confined to school settings, but are typical of the broader experiences of public servants seeking to meet *all* needs in a plural democratic society, and their analysis has significant implications in all aspects of public life. Analysis of the dilemmas has illuminated the challenge: schools are charged with a substantial moral responsibility, to educate future citizens in complex judgement, informed by virtuous dispositions cultivated within the community. Where those in the school community see the school as essentially concerned with the transmission of specific skills of value to the individual in making his or her own choices, a 'moral community' model of schooling is unlikely to work well. Politics needs to recognise these tensions and work with them, by providing the public space within which these challenges and differences can be discussed and acceptable solutions found.

In education, child protection regulations are a good example of such politics in action. A generation ago, few local authorities in Scotland had defined processes for dealing with situations where it was suspected in a school that a child was at risk, for example a suspicion that the child was being sexually abused by another family member. There was consequently substantial room for discretionary choice by the headteacher in deciding how to respond to cases and doubtless many headteachers at the time experienced such situations as dilemmas – they perceived that the way in which they responded individually would determine the outcome and that the burden of that decision lay with them. Now, however, every authority in Scotland has clearly established procedures, child protection staff trained in these routines in each school and a clear definition of circumstances, decisions and referral. The headteacher is under instruction and must follow these processes – there is very little room for discretionary choice. What was a dilemma has become a technical practice – to follow the requirements laid down in statute and/or employer regulations, requirements established through the development of social and political consensus. Individual headteachers who have principled ethical objections to this approach would have to resign.

Such debates about the criteria and values which should apply to the service need to be played out on a public political stage. The public service professional who understands the 'sharp end' of the service could usefully participate in that wider debate, contributing their understanding to the public discussion. However, public employers in the UK may prevent their employees from speaking out directly to the public, so that headteachers such as the one involved in Vignette 2 feel frustrated and disempowered professionally as they are unable to 'serve' the public as they would wish by contributing their specialist insight to the public debate. Typically in the UK the 'voice of the profession' then comes through professional bodies rather than individuals.[2] At the macropolitical level of governmental decision-making this voice becomes one of many contributing to debate and policy. In the more complex microlevel, such as schools, where decisions affect individuals, the rules of engagement and political accountabilities of different public service professions vary greatly, as do the opportunities afforded for contribution to public debate. For some professions, as widely varying as planners and doctors, professional ethical standards support decision making and protect the professional from political influence. The influence of the politician on the public service professional is restricted by the professional code of ethics. This is essential where public service professionals are, among other roles, acting as resource gatekeepers, making decisions about who will get what service in a context of limited resources and limitless demand. In market models of professional service, individuals who can afford to do so are able to choose services (including schooling) which suit their preferences. Often the solution to a dilemma is to opt out and go elsewhere. In public service, the element of choice (which allows for diversity) may be restricted through, for example, resource allocation decisions being made across a whole region, not at individual level, or through difficulties in providing the fine-grained individualised service which might be needed for a particular situation. These problems run right through current difficulties in the UK with the National Health Service or our community's responses to the care needs of older people. These considerations require a reconceptualisation of the role of the public service professional and his or her engagement with political processes.

It is not common to see politics portrayed as a noble ethical art, with politicians struggling on behalf of all of us to make sense of the complexities of a contested civic space. Yet consideration of the dilemmas of the headteacher, and public service more generally, suggests that politicians as individuals (elected public servants) and political parties (people grouped round a set of common compromises) both have an ethical role. As those charged with making the decisions within which skilled professionals are called to act, they might struggle with dilemmas more than anyone else. However, adversarial decision making, or contests in which there is a winner and a loser, have been characteristic of much UK politics. In the adversarial model, it is not necessary to reach a compromise with your opponent, nor to acknowledge the underlying complexity represented by the two competing views. Adversaries don't have dilemmas. They win or they lose. The linear rationality used by the media and in much public debate in UK politics often implies that one part of a complex situation can be answered without disadvantaging another. Of course, politics is about conflicts of interests, and how these can best be resolved. Majority voting, with protection for the rights of minority groups and the civil liberties of the individual, provides a widely accepted institutional framework for allowing clear decisions while protecting against the abuse of power. However, political institutions in the early twenty-first century struggle with the bigger challenges of including every citizen, or responding to every need, while balancing the two great democratic principles of freedom (too much of which creates great inequality) and equality (the imposition of which restricts freedom). This is true at the macro level of national government, and this book has argued that it is true also at the micro level of the school. Etzioni (1997), a clear advocate of a communitarian approach, argues against crude adversarial politics. His idealistic vision involves developing respectful decision-making through community-wide involvement in debate ('megalogues'), with an eye to key principles of democratic living (safety, dignity, respect, inclusion). It is hard to see macrosocial institutional responses to Etzioini's challenge in a society such as the UK where the tone of political debate owes as much to the tabloid press as to respectful dialogue between different views and where there are massive apparently irreconcilable differences between individuals and groups about the some of the most important issues in people's lives, such as sexual morality.

The debate generated by such issues is not peculiar to schools. It is a social debate about how we come to terms with plurality and is at the heart of many contemporary political and social problems. It is seen, for example, in the deep resentment, expressed in a variety of international guises, which some of the guardians of Muslim culture have for the invasive character of market-based, technologically dominant individualist approaches to morality. Can we move beyond the 'lowest common denominator' approach, within which the best we can do is to provide a neutral space within which to debate our differences and resolve them collectively (though often that seems enough of a challenge)? Is it possible to use the neutral space to work towards a 'highest common factor' in our understanding of the challenges we face in our lives, individually and collectively? A starting-point must be to develop a shared vocabulary, a shared set of concepts, for making sense of the complexity we face. The dilemmas of schooling show just how difficult that task is, but also the possibility of facing it and working at it each in our location, 'from the bottom up'. Where better to start than in schools themselves? And if we are to face up to these challenges in schools, let us have the resources, moral, conceptual and physical, to do so.

This is where I feel that I am professionally now. I am headteacher of a school which fully represents a wide range of the pluralities of modern living and which lacks a shared set of conceptual tools with which to make sense of the disorderly and challenging character of many of the exchanges which result. Despite a much improved policy framework for education in

Scotland over the past few years, individuals still experience difficulty and tension when they encounter the fault lines which fracture our society into many pieces; many individual children, growing up in social and relational complexity, find it hard to anchor their lives in secure cognitive and emotional understandings of where they fit in. The dilemmas do not go away, they only change their outward characteristics. In seeking to work with the parents, staff, children of the school, to make a meaningful and purposeful common life together, I am no less challenged, and in many ways more challenged, than ever before in my professional life, particularly since the gap between our expectations (limitless) and our resources (limited) has never been wider. It is, nonetheless, a welcome challenge, a challenge accepted by headteachers and teachers throughout the country, a challenge realised in the daily exchanges that result from the dilemmas of schooling.

If, as has been argued throughout this study, schools are a place where the political desire for social order meets with the complex reality of a fragmenting plural society, then the challenge of schools is the challenge of democracy. A leading Swedish educator has described education in democracy as 'inoculation against fascism' (Ekholm, 2002). In the rich, growing economies of the early twenty-first century, it is easy to see fascism as a remote product of a bygone age. As wealth increases, the citizens of rich societies can insulate themselves from compromise through exercising individual choice. But what happens if wealth dries up and choices are restricted? Can we provide the citizens of the future with the resources to interpret and evaluate together the difficult social, political, ethical and environmental challenges they will face? This is not just a question of understanding, but of action: the creative action of those who work in our schools and which builds the bonds of social trust through good intention and shared dialogue. It is a challenge to build the bonds of community afresh, rather than settle for the restricted individualist morality of choice, in which each seeks an individual pathway. It is a challenge which we can only address through building a sense of common purpose in our lives in community together, where we address with each other, in a disciplined and respectful way, the questions that matter in our lives and for the future our children will inherit.

Notes

1 For a good discussion of an independent control study of the ethical development of medical students see Myyry and Helkama (2002). For similar discussion of the ethical development of law students see Hartwell 1995. Keefer and Ashley (2001) discuss the ethical skills needed for successful professional practice, using medical and engineering examples.

2 A notable recent exception, which may prefigure further change in this area, was the unprecedented and very public criticism of current UK government policy on Iraq by the serving Head of the British Army, General Sir Richard Dannatt in October 2006.

REFERENCES

Aitchison. J. (2002) *The Articulate Mammal*, London: Routledge

Apple, M. W. and Beane, J. A. (eds) (1999) *Democratic Schools: Lessons from the Chalkface*, Buckingham: Open University Press

Argyris, C. (1990), *Overcoming Organisational Defences*, Boston: Allyn and Bacon

Aronson, E. (1980) *The Social Animal*, San Francisco: W. H. Freeman

Ashbaugh, C. and Kasten, K. (1984) 'A typology of operant values in school administration', *Planning and Changing*, Vol. 15, No. 4, pp. 195–208

Barker, B. (1999) 'Double vision: 40 years on', Chapter 7 in Tomlinson *et al.* (eds) (1999)

Bauman, Z. (1993) *Postmodern Ethics*, Oxford: Blackwell

Bauman, Z. (2001) *The Individualised Society*, Cambridge: Polity Press

Beatty, B. (2000a) 'The Paradox of emotion and educational leadership', paper presented at the British Educational Administration and Management Annual Conference, Bristol, 2000

Beatty, B. (2000b) 'Pursuing the paradox of emotion and educational leadership' (online), presentation in the Australian Principals Association Online Conference 2000. Available from URL: www.beecoswebengine.org/cache13/Con2000_wk2_Beatty1.html on (accessed 3 January 2007)

Beatty, B. and Brew, C. (2004) 'Trusting relationships and emotional epistemologies', *School Leadership and Management*, Vol. 24, No. 3, pp. 329–56

Beck, L. G. and Murphy, J. (1997) *Ethics in Educational Leadership Programs: Emerging Models*, Columbus, MO: University Council for Educational Administration

Begley, P. (ed.) (1999a) *Values and Educational Leadership*, Albany, NY: State University of New York Press

Begley, P. (1999b) 'Value preferences, ethics and conflicts', Chapter 12 in Begley (ed.) (1999a)

Begley, P. (ed.) (2004a) Special Issue on 'Understanding and responding ethically to the dilemmas of school based leadership', *International Studies in Educational Administration* Vol. 32, No. 2.

Begley, P. (2004b) 'Understanding valuation processes: exploring the linkage between motivation and action', in Begley (ed.) (2004a), pp. 4–17

Begley, P. and Johansson, O. (eds) (2003) *The Ethical Dimensions of School Leadership*, Dordrecht: Kluwer Academic Publishers

Begley, P. and Leonard, P. (1999) *The Values of Educational Administration*, London: Falmer Press

Best, D. (1999) 'The arts, morality and postmodernism', Chapter 12 in Halstead, J. and McLaughlin, T. (1999) *Education in Morality*, London: Routledge

Billot, J. (2003) 'The real and the ideal: the role and workload of secondary principals in New Zealand', *International Studies in Educational Administration*, Vol. 31, No. 1, pp. 33–49

Blase, J. and Anderson, G. (1995) *The Micropolitics of Educational Leadership: From Control to Empowerment*, London: Cassell

Bottery, M. (1998) *Professionals and Policy: Management Strategy in a Competitive World*, London: Cassell

Bottery, M. (2003) 'The management and mismanagement of trust', *Educational Management and Administration*, Vol. 31, No. 3, pp. 245–62

Bransford, J. and McCarrell, N. (1974) 'A sketch of a cognitive approach to understanding', Chapter 10 in Weimer, W. and Palermo, D. (eds) (1974) *Cognition and the Symbolic Process*, Hillsdale, NJ: Lawrence Erlbaum

Bryk, A. and Schneider, B. (2002) *Trust in Schools*, New York: Russell Sage

Callahan, J. (1988) *Ethical Issues in Professional Life*, Oxford: Oxford University Press

Campbell, E. (1992) 'Personal morals and organisational ethics: how teachers and principals cope with conflicting values in the context of school cultures', PhD thesis, Toronto, Institute of Education

Campbell, E. (1996) 'Suspended morality and the denial of ethics: how value relativism muddles the distinction between right and wrong in administrative decisions, Chapter 5 in Jacobson *et al.* (eds) (1996)

Campbell, E. (2000) 'Professional ethics in teaching; towards the development of a code of practice', *Cambridge Journal of Education*, Vol. 30, No. 2, pp. 203–21

Campbell, E. (2003) 'Let right be done; trying to put ethical standards into practice', in Begley and Johansson (eds) (2003), pp. 101–25

Cannon-Bowers, J. and Salas, E. (eds) (2000) *Making Decisions Under Stress: Implications for Individual and Team Training*, Washington, DC: American Psychological Association

Cardno, C. (1997) 'Problem based methodology in leadership development: interventions to improve dilemma management' (online), paper presented at the Australian Association for Research in Education Conference 1997. Available from URL: www.aare.ed.u.au/97pap/cardc337.htm on (accessed 26 June 2003)

Carr, A. (1994) 'The "emotional fallout" of the new efficiency movement in public administration in Australia: a case study', *Administration and Society*, Vol. 26, No. 3, pp. 344–58

Carr, D. (2000) 'Education, profession and culture: some conceptual questions', Inaugural Lecture delivered at the University of Edinburgh Faculty of Education, March 2000

Carr, D. (2002) 'Moral education and the perils of developmentalism',*Journal of Moral Education* Vol. 31, No. 1, pp. 5–19

Carr, D. and Landon, J. (1998) 'Teachers and schools as agencies of values education: reflections on teachers' perceptions part I: the role of the teacher',*The Journal of Beliefs and Values*, Vol. 19, No. 2, pp. 165–76

Carr, D. and Landon, J. (1999) 'Teachers and schools as agencies of values education: reflections on teachers' perceptions part II: the hidden curriculum',*The Journal of Beliefs and Values*, Vol. 20, No. 1, pp. 21–9

Chambers, J. (2003) *Sociolinguistic Theory*, Oxford: Blackwell

Chaplain, R. (2001) 'Stress and job satisfaction among primary headteachers: a question of balance',*Educational Management and Administration*, Vol. 29, No. 2, pp. 197–215

Clauser, K. and Gert, B. (1990) 'A critique of principilism',*Journal of Medicine and Philosophy*, Vol. 15, pp. 219–36

Coleman, J. (1988) 'Social capital in the creation of human capital',*American Journal of Sociology*, Vol. 94, Supplement, pp. 95–120

COSLA (Convention of Scottish Local Authorities) (n d) TAC Team Collegiality Toolkit (online). Available from URL: www.scottishcouncils.org/tact/ (accessed 3 Jan 2007)

Cooper, C. and Kelly, M. (1993) 'Occupational stress in headteachers: a national UK study',*British Journal of Educational Psychology*, Vol. 63, No. ??, pp. 130–43

Cowie, M. (2001) *Talking Heads: A Critical Analysis of the Quality Assurance Relationship between Secondary Schools and an Education Authority*, Aberdeen: Centre for Educational Research: University of Aberdeen

Cranston, N., Ehrich, L. and Billot, J. (2003) 'The secondary school principalship in

Australia and New Zealand: an investigation of changing roles',*Leadership and Policy in Schools*, Vol. 2, No. 3, pp. 159–88

Croxford, L. (2001)'Comprehensive schools in Great Britain: evidence from research', unpublished paper, University of Edinburgh: Centre for Educational Sociology

Cuban, L. (1992) 'Managing dilemmas while building professional communities',*Educational Researcher*, Vol. 21, No. 1, pp. 4–11

Cuban, L. (1996) 'Reforming the practice of educational administration through managing dilemmas', Chapter 1 in Jacobson *et al.* (eds) (1996)

Day, C., Harris, A., Hadfield, M., Tolley, H. and Bereseford, J. (2000) 'School leadership: tensions and dilemmas',*Leading Schools in Times of Change*, Buckingham: Open University Press

Dearden, R. F. (1968) *The Philosophy of Primary Education*, London: Routledge and Kegan Paul

Dempster, N. and Berry, V. (2003) 'Blindfolded in a minefield: principals' ethical decision making',*Cambridge Journal of Education*, Vol. 33, No. 3, pp. 457–77

Dempster, N. and Mahony, P. (1998) 'Ethical challenges in school leadership',Chapter 8 in MacBeath (1998)

Dempster, N., Carter. L., Freakley, M. and Parry, L. (2004) 'Contextual influences on school leaders in Australia: some data from a recent study of principals' ethical decision-making',*School Leadership and Management*, Vol. 24, No. 2, pp. 163–74

Dempster, N., Freakley, M. and Parry, L. (2002) 'Professional development for school principals in ethical decision making',*Journal of In-Service Education*, Vol. 28, No. 3, pp. 427–46

Derry, S. (1996) 'Cognitive schema in the constructivist debate',*Educational Psychologist* Vol. 31, No. 3/4, pp. 163–74

Donaldson, M. (1992) *Human Minds*, London: Allen Lane The Penguin Press

Duignan, P. (2001) 'The managed heart',*Improving Schools*, Vol. 4, No. 3, pp. 33–9

Duignan, P. and Collins, V. (2001) 'Leadership challenges and ethical dilemmas in frontline service organisations', paper presented at the British Educational Research Association Annual Conference, Leeds

Duignan, P. and Collins, V. (2003) 'Leadership challenges and ethical dilemmas in front-line organisations', in Bennett, N., Crawford, M. and Cartwright, M. (eds) (2003) *Effective Educational Leadership*, London: Open University Press in association with Paul Chapman Publishing

Dunne, J. (1993) *Back to the Rough Ground: 'Phronesis'and 'Techne' in Modern Philosophy and Aristotle*, Notre Dame, IN: University of Notre Dame Press

Ehrich, L., Cranston, N. and Kimber, M. (2004) 'Public sector managers and ethical dilemmas',*Journal of Australian and New Zealand Academy of Management*, Vol. 10, No. 1, pp. 25–37

Ehrich, L., Cranston, N. and Kimber, M.(2006) 'Ethical dilemmas: the "bread and butter" of educational leaders' lives', *Journal of Educational Administration*, Vol. 44, No. 3, pp. 106–21

Ekholm, M. (2002) 'To make schools democratic: a long term commitment', paper presented at the Commonwealth Council for Educational Administration and Management conference, *Exploring New Horizons in School Leadership for Democratic Schools*, Umea, Sweden

Eraut, M. (1994) *Professional Knowledge and Competence*, London: Falmer Press

Etzioni, A. (1997) *The New Golden Rule: Community and Morality in a Democratic Society*, London: Profile Books

Evans, L. (1989) 'Some causes of bias in expert opinion',*The Psychologist*, Vol. 2, No. 2, pp. 12–114

Evans, L. (2001) 'Delving deeper into morale, job satisfaction and motivation among education professionals',*Educational Management and Administration*, Vol. 29, No. 2, pp. 291–306

Fish, D. and Coles, C. (1998), *Developing Professional Judgement in Health Care*, Oxford: Butterworth Heinemann

Fisher, R., Ury, W. and Patton, B. (1989) *Getting to Yes*, London: Business Books

Forsyth, P., Barnes, L. and Adams, C. (2006) 'Trust effectiveness patterns in schools',*Journal of Educational Administration*, Vol. 44, No. 2, pp. 122–41

Fullan, M. (2003) *Change Forces with a Vengeance*, London: Falmer

Furman, G. (2004) 'The ethic of community',*Journal of Educational Administration*, Vol. 42, No. 2, pp. 215–35

Garland, D. (2002) *The Culture of Control*, Oxford: Oxford University Press

Gilligan, C. (1982) *In a Different Voice: Psychological Theory and Women's Development* Cambridge, MA: Harvard University Press

Goddard, T. (2004) 'The role of school leaders in establishing democratic principles in a post-conflict society',*Journal of Educational Administration*, Vol. 42, No. 6, pp. 685–96

Goleman, D. (2003) *The New Leaders: Emotional Intelligence at Work*, London: Little, Brown

Goleman, D., Boyatzis, R. and McKee, A. (2002)*The New Leadership: Emotional Intelligence at Work*, London: Little, Brown

Greenfield, W. (2004) 'Moral leadership in schools',*Journal of Educational Administration*, Vol. 42, No. 2, pp. 174–96

Grace, G. (1995) *School Leadership: Beyond Education Management*, London: Falmer Press

Grace, G. (2002) *Catholic Schools: Mission, Markets and Morality*, London: Routledge Falmer

Grogan, M. and Smith, F. (1999) 'A feminist perspective of woman superintendents' approach to moral dilemmas', Chapter 14 in Begley (ed.) (1999a), pp. 273–88

Gronn, P. (2003) *The New Work of Educational Leaders*, London: Paul Chapman Publishing

Habermas, J. (1986) *Autonomy and Solidarity*,London: Verso

Hallinger, P. and Bridges, E. (1994) 'Problem based learning in educational administration', *Studies in Educational Administration*, Vol. 39, pp. 15–23

Hamilton, L. (2002) 'Constructing pupil identity: personhood and ability',*British Educational Research Journal*, Vol. 28, No. 4, pp. 591–602

Hartwell, S. (1995) 'Promoting moral development through experiential teaching',*Clinical Law Review*, Vol. 1, No. 1, pp. 505–38

Hayward B., Mortimer, E. and Brunwin, T (2004) 'Survey of public attitudes towards conduct in public life' (online). Available at www.public-standards.gov.uk/research_ projects.aspx (accessed 5 January 2007)

HMI (Her Majesty's Inspectors of Schools) (1988) *Effective Secondary Schools*, Edinburgh: HMSO

HMI (Her Majesty's Inspectors of Schools) (1989) *Effective Primary Schools*, Edinburgh: HMSO

HMI (Her Majesty's Inspectors of Schools) (1996) *How Good Is Our School?*, Edinburgh: Scottish Office Education and Industry Department

Hochschild, S. R. (1983) *The Managed Heart: Commercialisation of Human Feeling*, Los Angeles: University of California Press

Hodgkinson, C. (1983) *The Philosophy of Leadership*, Oxford: Blackwell

Hood, C. (1991) 'A public management for all seasons?' *Public Administration*, Vol. 69, pp. 3–20

Hoy W. and Kupersmith W. (1984) 'Principal authenticity and faculty trust', *Planning and Change*, Vol. 15, No. 2, pp. 80–8

Hursthouse, R. (2001) *On Virtue Ethics*, Oxford: Oxford University Press

Hutton, W. (1995) *The State We're In*, London: Jonathan Cape

Jacobson, S., Hickcox, E. and Stevenson, R. (eds) (1996) *School Administration: Persistent Dilemmas in Preparation and Practice*, Westport, CN: Praeger

James, C. and Vince, R. (2001) 'Developing the leadership capabilities of headteachers', *Educational Management and Administration*, Vol. 29, No. 3, pp. 307–17

Janis, I. (1972) *Victims of Groupthink*, Boston: Houghton, Mifflin

Johansson, O. (2004a) 'A democratic, learning and communicative leadership' *Journal of Educational Administration*, Vol. 42, No. 6, pp. 697–707

Johansson, O. (2004b) 'Democracy and leadership – or training for democratic leadership', *Journal of Educational Administration*, Vol. 42, No. 6, pp. 620–4

Johnson, C. (2001) *Meeting the Ethical Challenges of Leadership: Casting Light or Shadows*, Thousand Oaks, CA: Sage

Johnson, H., McCreery, E. and Castelli, M. (2000) 'The role of the headteacher in developing children holistically: perspectives from Anglicans and Catholics', *Educational Management and Administration*, Vol. 28, No. 4, pp. 389–403

Kakabadse, A. and Kakabadse, N. (1999) *Essence of Leadership*, London: International Thompson Business Press

Keefer, M. and Ashley, K. 'Case-based approaches to professional ethics: a systematic comparison of students' and ethicists' moral reasoning' *Journal of Moral Education*, Vol. 30, No. 4, pp. 377–97

Keil, F. and Wilson, R. (1999) *Explanation and Cognition*, Cambridge, MA: MIT Press

Kidder, R. (2003) *How Good People Make Tough Choices: Resolving the Dilemmas of Ethical Living*, New York: HarperCollins Quill

Kilpatrick, W. (1993) *Why Johnny Can't Tell Right from Wrong*, New York: Simon & Schuster

Kolb, D. (1984) *Experiential Learning*, Englewood Cliffs, NJ: Prentice-Hall

Lam, Y. (1996) 'Principals' dilemmas: intraorganisational demands and environmental boundary spanning activities', Chapter 10 in S. Jacobson *et al.* (eds) (1996)

Larmore, C. (1987) *Patterns of Moral Complexity*, Cambridge: Cambridge University Press

Lawrence, J. (1999) *Arguments for Action: Ethics and Professional Conduct*, Aldershot: Ashgate

Lawton, S. (2006) 'The role of educational choice in facilitating diversity and maintaining unity', *International Studies in Educational Administration*, Vol. 34, No. 1, pp. 21–33

Levinson, S. (2003) *Space in Language and Cognition: Explorations in Cognitive Diversity*, Cambridge: Cambridge University Press

Lind, G. (2006) 'Moral Judgement Test' (online). Available from URL: www.uni-konstanz. de/ag-moral/mut/mjt-engl.htm (accessed 3 January 2007)

Little, A. (1997) *Managing Change – the Australian Experience: Survey Results*, Sydney: Arthur D. Little International

Loader, D. (1997) *The Inner Principal*, London: Falmer Press

Lunt, I. and Norwich, B. (1999) *Can Effective Schools be Inclusive Schools?* London: Institute of Education, University of London

MacBeath, J. (ed.) (1998) *Effective School Leadership: Responding to Change*, London: Paul Chapman

MacIntyre, A. (1981) *After Virtue: A Study in Moral Theory*, London: Duckworth

MacIntyre, A. (1988) *Whose Justice? Which Rationality?*, London: Duckworth

MacIntyre, A. (1990) *Three Rival Versions of Moral Enquiry*, London: Duckworth

Mackenzie, H. (1995) *Craigroyston Days: The Story of an Educational Revolution*, Edinburgh: Mainstream

Mahony, P., MacBeath, J. and Moos, L. (1998) 'Who really runs the school?' Chapter 7 in MacBeath (ed.) (1998)

Mandler, J. (1984) *Stories, Scripts and Scenes: Aspects of Schema Theory*, Hillsdale, NJ: Lawrence Erlbaum

Marshall, S. (1995) *Schemas in Problem Solving*, Cambridge: Cambridge University Press

Martin, R. (2002) *The Responsibility Virus*, New York: Basic Books

McEwen, A., McClune, B. and Knipe, D. (2000) 'Management and values: the changing role of the secondary headteacher', *Teacher Development*, Vol. 4, No. 2, pp. 223–40

McFall, L. (1998) 'Fictional truth', Chapter 6 in Carr, D. (ed.) (1998) *Education, Knowledge and Truth*, London: Routledge

McNulty, P. (2005) *Extreme Headship*, Oxford: Trafford Publishing

Mercer, D. (1996) 'Can they walk on water? Professional isolation and the secondary headteacher', *School Organisation*, Vol. 16, No. 2, pp. 165–78

Mintzberg, H. (1975) 'The manager's job: folklore and fact',*Harvard Business Review*, Vol. 53, No. 4, pp. 49–61

Moller, J. (1996) 'Reframing educational leadership in the perspective of dilemmas', Chapter 16 in Jacobson *et al.* (eds) (1996)

Moller, J. (2002) 'Democratic leadership in an age of managerial accountability', keynote address at the Commonwealth Council for Educational Administration and Management conference, *Exploring New Horizons in School Leadership for Democratic Schools*, Umea, Sweden

Moore, R. and Young, M. (2001) 'Knowledge and the curriculum in the sociology of education: towards a reconceptualisation',*British Journal of Sociology of Education*, Vol. 22, No. 4, pp. 445–61

Moos, L. and Dempster, N. (1998) 'Comparative learnings from the study', Chapter 6 in MacBeath (ed.) (1998)

Moos, L. and Moller, J. (2003) 'Schools and leadership in transition: the case of Scandinavia', *Cambridge Journal of Education*, Vol. 33, No. 3, pp. 353–70

Mulford, B. (2004) 'Congruence between the democratic purposes of schools and school principal training in Australia', *Journal of Educational Administration*, Vol. 42, No. 6, pp. 625–39

Murphy, D. (1999) 'A strong vision fatally weakened', *The Herald* (Glasgow), 22 February

Murphy, D. (2002) 'Dilemmas of practice in leading Scottish comprehensive schools', paper presented at the Commonwealth Council for Educational Administration and Management conference, *Exploring New Horizons in School Leadership for Democratic Schools*, Umea, Sweden

Murphy, D. (2003) 'Scottish heads/deputes survey – May 2003: a summary report',*Bylines (Journal of the Headteachers Association of Scotland)* Vol. 17, No. 3, p. 23

Murphy, J. (2002) 'Reculturing the profession of educational leadership: new blueprints', *Education Administration Quarterly*, Vol. 38, No. 2, pp. 176–91

Myyry, L. and Helkama, K. (2002) 'The role of value priorities and professional ethics training in moral sensitivity',*Journal of Moral Education*, Vol. 31, No. 1, pp. 23–50

NCSL (National College of School Leadership) (n d) (online). Available from URL: www. ncsl.org.uk/research/research_associates/research-researchassociates-completed.cfm (accessed 3 January 2007)

Nielsen, R. P. (1996) *The Politics of Ethics*, New York: Oxford University Press

Noddings, N. (1992) *The Challenge to Care in Schools*, New York: Teachers College Press

Nussbaum, M. (1993) 'Non-relative virtues: an Aristotelian approach', in Nussbaum, M. and Sen, A. (eds) (1993) *The Quality of Life*, Oxford: Clarendon Press, pp. 242–69

O'Brien, J., Murphy, D. and Draper, J. (2003) *School Leadership*, Edinburgh: Dunedin Academic Press

Paterson, L. (1997a) 'Student achievement and educational change in Scotland 1980–1995', *Scottish Educational Review*, Vol. 29, No. 1, pp. 10–19

Paterson, L. (1997b) 'Individual autonomy and comprehensive education, *British Educational Research Journal*, Vol. 23, No. 3, pp. 315–27

Paterson, L. (2000) *Crisis in the Classroom*, Edinburgh: Mainstream

Pinker, S. (1998) *How the Mind Works*, London: Allen Lane The Penguin Press

RAE (Research Assessment Exercise) (n d) (online). Available from URL: www.rae.ac.uk (accessed 3 January 2007)

Rawls, J. (1971) *A Theory of Justice*, Cambridge, MA: Harvard University Press

Reeves, J., Forde, C., O'Brien, J., Smith, P. and Tomlinson, H. (2002), *Performance Management in Education: Improving Practice*, London: Paul Chapman Publishing

Rest, J. (1986) *Moral Development: Advances in Theory and Research*, New York: Praeger

Rest, J. and Narváez, D. (1994) *Moral Development in the Professions: Psychology and Applied. Ethics*, Hillsdale, NJ: Lawrence Earlbaum

Reyna, S. (2002) *Connections: Brain, Mind and Culture in Social Anthropology*, London: Routledge

Ribbins, P. and Marland, M. (1994) *Headship Matters*, Harlow: Longman

Rich, J. (1984) *Professional Ethics in Education*, Springfield, IL: Charles C. Thomas

Riley, K. (1998) *Whose School is it Anyway?*, London: Falmer Press

Riley, K. (2002) ' "Democratic leadership" – a contradiction in terms?', keynote address at the Commonwealth Council for Educational Administration and Management conference, *Exploring New Horizons in School Leadership for Democratic Schools*, Umea, Sweden

Roche, K. (1999) 'Moral and ethical dilemmas in Catholic school settings', Chapter 13 in Begley (ed.) (1999a)

Rossmore, D. (1989) 'Leader/consultant dilemmas: the primary barrier to satisficing',*Cons ultation*, Vol. 8, No. 1, pp. 3–24

Rothstein, B. (2003) 'Social capital, economic growth and quality of government: the causal mechanism', *New Political Economy*, Vol. 8, No. 1, pp. 49–71

Sadurski, W. (1990) *Moral Pluralism and Legal Neutrality*, Dordrecht: Kluwer Academic Publishers

Saville-Troike, M. (2003) *The Ethnography of Communication*, Oxford: Blackwell

Schein, E. (1985) *Organisational Culture and Management*, San Francisco: Jossey Bass

Schon, D. (1987) *Educating the Reflective Practitioner*, San Francisco: Jossey-Bass

Scottish Executive Education Dept (SEED) (2000a) 'Standards in Scotland's Schools etc Act' (online). Available from URL: www.scotland-legislation.hmso.gov.uk/legislation/Scotland/acts2000/20000006 (accessed 3 January 2007)

Scottish Executive Education Dept (2000b) 'The structure and balance of the curriculum 5–14' (online). Available from URL: www.ltscotland.org.uk/5to14/guidelines/structureandbalance.asp (accessed 5 January 2007)

Scottish Executive Education Dept (2001) 'A teaching profession for the 21st century' (online). Available from URL: www.scotland.gov.uk/library3/Education/tp21a-03.asp#3 (accessed 3 January 2007)

Scottish Executive Education Dept (2004) *Ambitious, Excellent Schools*, Edinburgh: SEED

Scottish Executive Education Dept (2005) 'The Standard for Headship in Scotland' (online). Available from URL: www.scotland.gov.uk/Publications/2005/11/3085829/58 300 (accessed 3 January 2007)

Scottish Executive Education Dept (n d) 'A Curriculum for Excellence' (online). Available from URL: www.acurriculumforexcellence.gov.uk (accessed 3 January 2007)

Senge, P., Cambron-McCabe, N., Lucas, T., Smith, B., Dutton, J. and Kleiner, A. (2000) *Schools That Learn*, London: Nicholas Brealey Publishing

Sergiovanni, T. (1994) *Building Community in Schools*, San Francisco: Jossey-Bass

Shapiro, J. and Stefkovich, J. (2001) *Ethical Leadership and Decision Making in Schools*, Mahwah, NJ: Lawrence Erlbaum

Shapiro, J. and Stefkovich, J. (2003) 'Deconstructing communities: educational leaders and their ethical decision-making processes', in Begley and Johansson (eds) (2003), pp. 89–106

Simon, H. (1957) *Models of Man*, New York: Wiley

Singh, B. (2000) 'Further attempts to balance liberal virtues with claims for cultural identity within traditional non-liberal communities', *Educational Studies*, Vol. 26, No. 2, pp. 213–28

Standards for School Leaders (2007) international webreferences are conveniently available from URL:beecoswebengine.org/cache13/LL_LEADERSHIP_STANDARDS. html (accessed 3 January 2007)

Starrat, R. (1994) *Building an Ethical School : A Practical Response to the Moral Crisis in Schools*, London, Falmer

Starrat, R. (2003) *Ethical Leadership*, San Francisco: Jossey-Bass

Starrat, R (2005) 'Cultivating the moral character of learning and teaching: a neglected dimension of educational leadership',*School Leadership and Management*, Vol. 25, No. 4, pp. 399–411

Statman, D. (ed.) (1997) *Virtue Ethics: A Critical Reader*, Edinburgh: Edinburgh University Press

Stefkovich, J. and O'Brien, G. (2004) 'Best interests of the student: an ethical model', *Journal of Educational Administration*, Vol. 42, No. 2, pp. 197–214

Sternberg, R. and Horvath, J. (1999) *Tacit Knowledge in Professional Practice: Research and Practitioner Perspectives*, Mahwah NJ: Lawrence Erlbaum

Strike, K., Haller, E. and Soltis, J. (1988) *The Ethics of School Administration*, New York: Teachers College Press

Thomson, A. (1999) *Critical Reasoning in Ethics: A Practical Introduction*, Routledge: London

Tomasello, M. (2001) 'Perceiving intentions and learning words in the second year of life', Chapter 5 in Bowerman, M. and Levinson, S. (eds) (2001) *Language Acquisition and Conceptual Development*, Cambridge: Cambridge University Press

Tomlinson, H., Gunter, H. and Smith, P. (eds) (1999) *Living Headship: Voices, Values and Vision*, London: Paul Chapman Publishing

Tripp, D. (1993) *Critical Incidents in Teaching*, London: Routledge

Tschannen-Moran, M. and Hoy, W. (1997) 'Trust in schools: a conceptual and empirical analysis', *Journal of Educational Administration*, Vol. 36, No. 4, pp. 334–52

Uleman, J. and Bargh, J. (1989) *Unintended Thought*, New York: Guilford Press

Vann, B. (1999) 'Micropolitics in the UK: can a principal ever be expected. to be one of us?',*School Leadership and Management*, Vol. 19, No. 2, pp. 201–4

Varela, F. (1999) *Ethical Know-How: Action, Wisdom and Cognition*, Palo Alto, CA: Stanford University Press

Vokey, D. (2001) *Moral Discourse in a Pluralistic World*, Notre Dame, IN: University of Notre Dame Press

Walker, K. and Shakotko, D. (1999) 'The Canadian superintendency: value-based challenges and pressures',Chapter 15 in Begley (ed.) (1999a)

Western Australia Dept of Education and Training (2004) 'Western Australia Standards for Principals' (online). Available from URL: isp.ecu.edu.au/ssl/index.php (accessed 3 January 2007)

Wildy, H. and Louden, W. (2000) 'school restructuring and the dilemmas of principals' work',*Educational Management and Administration*, Vol. 28 No. 2, pp. 173–84

Willower, D. (1999) 'Values and valuation', Chapter 6 in Begley (ed.) (1999a), pp. 121–38

Index